After losing his wife and children in the bombing of Air India Flight 182 on 23 June 1985, Dr. Chandrasekhar Sankurathri gave up his comfortable life and job in Canada, and returned to India to dedicate his life to serve the poor and needy in rural areas of Andhra Pradesh. Since then, he has established several charitable institutes, including a school and an eye hospital, in his relentless pursuit of bringing about the changes he wants in society.

His work has been covered widely in the media and in documentaries, and he has won several awards in India, Canada and the US for his humanitarian work.

A RAY OF HOPE

A Ray of Hope

Dr. Chandrasekhar Sankurathri

msmf.ca

The views and opinions expressed in this work are the author's own and the facts are as reported by her/him, and the publisher is in no way liable for the same.

Text Copyright © 2018 Chandrasekhar Sankurathri

All rights reserved

No part of this book may be reproduced, or stored in a retrieval system, or transmitted in any form or by any means, electronic, mechanical, photocopying, recording, or otherwise, without express written permission of the publisher.

Published by Westland Publications Private Limited
61, 2nd Floor, Silverline Building, Alapakkam Main Road,
Maduravoyal, Chennai 600095

Westland and the Westland logo are trademarks of
Westland Publications Private Limited, or its affiliates.

This book was researched and written by Bloody Good Book (division of Bushfire Publishers, a venture by Rashmi Bansal)

ISBN: 9789386850904

10 9 8 7 6 5 4 3 2 1

Typeset in Garamond Premier Pro by SÜRYA, New Delhi
Printed at Manipal Technologies Limited

CONTENTS

1. Life as a Small-town Boy   1
2. Discovering the Right Path   11
3. The Wonder Years   35
4. Turn of the Tide   51
5. Setting the Foundation for Sarada Vidyalayam   85
6. Braving All Odds   95
7. Forming a Vision   103
8. Fulfilling the Vision   111
9. The Way Forward   125
    How You Can Help   135

chapter one

Life as a Small-town Boy

Today, at seventy-two, when I jog down memory lane, bits and pieces of my childhood days float into consciousness. The sight of the flowing Godavari River, the smell of incense during early morning prayers at the temple my mother visited, the feel of rain-soaked soil beneath my bare feet as I romped around the playground with my friends, and the clanging of the brass plate as it slipped from my mother's hands as she collapsed in the courtyard. Growing up in the small town of Rajahmundry in the East Godavari district of Andhra Pradesh, I led a simple life. My childhood memories are bittersweet. The memories of love and friendship tinged with struggle, loss and pain.

I was born in 1943, the eleventh child of station master Appala Narasayya Naidu and his homemaker wife, Ramayamma. In spite of running an average income household, father (who I called Nanna) ensured that his six boys and five girls had a proper education and upbringing. Being employed with the British government, he was held in high regard by the townsfolk. Amma was a simple, kind and religious woman. I was quite close to her and tagged along wherever she went. The pair of us were a familiar sight at the nearby temples, which she visited regularly, as well as at the river bank during the month of Karthika. I clearly remember our neighbour's house, which stood on the banks of river Godavari.

One day, when I was at home with Amma, a neighbour called on her for a chat. As she stood talking, Amma suddenly collapsed, dropping the plate she was holding with a clang. She breathed her last right there. A flurry of activities followed her fall, but I was oblivious to them. At six years of age, all I could understand was that Amma was no more. In the days that followed, the memory of her face, her actions and her voice slowly faded away from my mind. All that remained was the strongly etched image of her dead body being prepared for the final journey of her life.

Realizing the gnawing gap that Amma's absence had left in my life, Nanna started paying more attention to me. I was in primary school then. After school he used to make me sit next to him, narrate stories and make me recite all the hundred verses from *Krishnashtakam*—poems about Lord Krishna—much to the amazement of family and acquaintances who wondered how I could recite all the poems so effortlessly. They would also compliment me and quiz me on my knowledge about movies. Although I rarely watched movies, I knew which films were showing at the cinemas and all the related details.

By the time I was eight, I started noticing that without Amma, my family had become like a rudderless ship. My father had already retired by then and was somehow managing the family affairs. Three of my brothers had completed their education—the eldest, Tulasi Rao, was a lawyer; the second, Venkata Appa Rau, was a lecturer; and the third, Venkat Rao, had a graduate degree in chemistry.

Starting School

My primary education was done at a Christian missionary school. I was fond of collecting the foreign stamps that the missionaries discarded. The school was close to home and I would walk to it with my best friend Raju (who is now Dr. V. K. Raju). We often wandered around on our way to and from the school, and used to hang around at the court buildings in the area. He also shared with me the goodies his mother made. We played football, kabbadi, kho-kho and cricket with other boys from the neighbourhood. Although I had other playmates, Raju was my only true friend. Our days were filled with fun, laughter, arguments and disagreements. I often called on Raju at his house, which was quite close to mine. His family was considered rich but that never made any difference to us. That was the best part of my life then—no prejudices about the rich and the poor, or discrimination between one caste and another. It was an easy-going life. We never owned any property or house, and so we were constantly moving from place to place. As a result, I have lived in several houses in Rajahmundry.

When I joined the Municipal High School in Class 5, Raju got into the Government Training College School in Class 4. But the change in schools didn't hamper our evening playtime together. Nanna had asked one of his nephews to get my admission done in a high school for Class 3. In those days, the schools had entrance exams for every grade. Instead of making me appear for the Class 3 entrance test, I was made to go for the Class 5 one. I cleared the test and was qualified to enter Class 5. Nobody thought anything about this omission and I got admission into Class 5. That's how I skipped two classes and moved ahead of my classmates and even my elder sister. Although people discussed this, I never had any regrets about skipping two classes. However, I wasn't quite happy at high school. When I was in Class 7 or 8, my father moved in with my brother Narayana Rao, while I, along with four of my siblings, started living with my eldest sister and her husband. We were bereft of many things and learnt to take each day as it came. Life had thrown us into a turbulent sea and we held on desperately to each other to stay afloat.

Life on the River Bed

Recently, while watching the coverage of the Chennai floods, my mind flew back to the monsoon of 1953 when Rajahmundry was besieged by floods. The Godavari river had always played a pivotal role in our lives as our house was quite close to its bund. It was a part of our celebrations, prayers and social life. But on 15 August 1953, the river took on the avatar of an angry goddess. Being a holiday, we were excited about the rising water levels of the Godavari and went to look at the waves of brownish water sloshing over the bund. Little did we know that the river was getting ready to douse us with her wrath. As we lay asleep that night, we heard panic-stricken voices waking us up and hustling us out of the house.

We were made to walk barefoot on a gravelled road all the way to an acquaintance's house, which was relatively safe. The next morning, when I looked out, I saw all the nearby houses were submerged under a sheet of water. I was too young to understand the loss that the flood had caused. It took three–four days for the water to recede. When we got back to our house, it was filled with clay and filth. Every possession was coated in clay. Immediately, the mopping operation began. Each one of us was involved in cleaning up the house. I don't remember how long it took to make the place habitable again, but it was one gruesome experience. At that time, we had some monetary help from my brother Venkat Rao. But to live in the aftermath of the floods, with barely any money, was an ordeal.

For us kids, life went on as usual. But behind all the games, laughter and camaraderie was the grim reality of the task of survival. And it was indeed a task! From a child's perspective, I could see that making both ends meet was far from easy for the grown-ups. I couldn't fully comprehend the struggles of the adult world, but I knew what hunger, suffering and poverty were.

Dealing with Another Loss

Amma's death had slipped out of my conscious mind as I was only six years old then. I was nine when Nanna passed away in 1953. He was at my brother's place when he had a paralytic stroke. He fell down on his way to the bathroom. He remained in coma for a few days before succumbing to his illness. Although I remember details about his last days, I wasn't psychologically affected by his death. Between 1950 and 1952, Nanna had been my mentor. He used to sit with me, narrate stories, answer my questions and ask me about my school and studies. He had the habit of giving me a few coins as pocket money. In spite of the financial strain he was going through, he never showed anger or despair. That's the kind of graceful man he was. Unfortunately, beyond those two years, I don't remember much about him.

At around the same time, my second brother, Dr. Rau, qualified for IAS examination. He was supposed to go for his viva when he was informed that he was banned from appearing for exams due to some complaint against him from the local college principal. The UPSC board called him for an explanation about this complaint. A strong, self-respecting man, Dr. Rau refused to go for the hearing and as a result was not able to get a posting. He found it difficult to continue living at Rajahmundry. One day, he walked out on all of us. No one knew where he was. Apparently, he had gone somewhere in the north of India and it was a while before he got back in touch with the family.

In 1956, I completed my SSLC course (high school diploma) and started with the intermediate course. All this while, I was in touch with Raju who remained my constant companion. He shifted to Vishakhapatnam (then known as Waltair) to study medicine. I, too, moved away from Rajahmundry to pursue further studies. I made it a point to meet him at Waltair as often as possible. During one of my lean periods, I had to borrow money from him to pay my fees. He was kind enough to lend me the amount, which I eventually returned. Our association, friendship and communication continued for a long time. Raju played an important part in my life when I relocated to India. Our friendship went through many ups and lows, which I will narrate during the course of the book.

Till 1956, I carried on with my life with the best of spirits and making the most of what I had. My education was on the right track and having lost my parents at a young age, I had learnt to deal with loss. But in that particular year, I felt such a blow that all the steadfastness of my nature went askew.

Amongst my siblings who took me under their wings, one was Padma. I was quite attached to her. She was warm, friendly and beautiful. Everyone admired her and were taken in by her good manners and pleasant demeanour. Her gentleness and kind words helped me deal with many of my growing up pains. In 1956, she was in her late teens. One day, quite suddenly, she committed suicide. Her death came as a violent blow to me. It was something I couldn't comprehend. I cried and cried, trying to figure out what had gone wrong, why she had taken such a drastic step. But there were no answers. At times, I blamed myself for her death—for not foreseeing something like this, for not doing enough for her, for not averting her death in whichever way possible. For days on end, I remained inconsolable. To own the truth, Padma's death left a scar on my consciousness that remained with me till my wedding with Manjari in 1975.

Padma was studying at Government College and her entire class turned up to offer condolences at our house. But the love the world showed for her was not enough. She was gone forever, and I was left with another loss to deal with. The following month, I had my exams. Without the least inclination to study, I prepared for the exams. I wrote my papers in a daze. Although I passed the examination while the rest of my classmates failed at it, I remained in a state of inertia, yearning for Padma to smile back at me, acknowledging my success.

A Ray of Hope

All these experiences added to my understanding of the vicious circle of poverty. I have long understood how natural disasters affect the life, plight and feelings of refugees: how they survive in camps, how children suffer when their parents are taken away from them. Having suffered losses at an early age, I could identify and empathize with the losses others faced, including strangers. It is possible that these experiences turned me into an introvert and a diffident person. I was not able to fully realize my capabilities. Had it not been for my brother Venkat Rao and his wife Kausalya, I would have been totally lost. She filled my life with motherly love. It's only because of her love and attention that I am what I am today. As soon as he got married, Venkat Rao took up a place in Rajahmundry and the four of us (two brothers and two sisters), who were living at our sister's place, moved in with them. My sister-in-law was a God-fearing person and she immediately took us all under her loving care. With her, we found a home and a mother. She and my brother got us educated and supported us, till we were independent.

Thereafter, my life changed for the better. But it took a long time for me to be more self-accepting and confident. I will not wish the experiences I had in my early childhood on any other child. Losses, poverty and dependency hit the self-esteem of a child and most often lead to a lack of purpose in life. I was lucky enough to have survived these daunting experiences. The love and support of my brother and his wife helped pull me and my siblings out of the mire of despondency that we were thrown into. I remain forever grateful to them for giving my life a direction and purpose and, most importantly, for filling it up with love.

chapter two

Discovering the Right Path

It's close to midnight and I am stranded at the airport. A dense fog has forced the authorities to cancel all flights. I pull my jacket tightly around me, trying to draw warmth and comfort from it. And perhaps some reassurance that everything will be alright.

It was my first trip abroad, my first hour in Canada, my first step towards higher education ... and all of it lay wrapped up in a blanket of fog. When I look back, this memory always pops up in my head. But I am breaking the linear flow of the story here. Let me go back to my college days in India and recount the incidents that led to that momentous night at Gander, Canada.

In 1956, I joined Government Art College, Rajahmundry, for my intermediate level. I had opted for Biology, Physics and Chemistry as subjects of specialization. I was all of thirteen years old then. College was a completely different experience. The medium changed from Telugu to English, and I was thrown into a class full of students who were in their late teens. Fortunately, I was able to make friends with a couple of them.

I had always dreamt of becoming a doctor. I remember that I used to scribble 'Dr. S. Chandrasekhar' in my notebooks. But by the time I passed my intermediate, I realized that I was too young to apply for medicine. The minimum age was seventeen and I was only fifteen at that time.

So, I decided to apply for a B.Sc. Honours degree in Botany. However, my brother suggested that Zoology had better job prospects, so through his reference I got into B.Sc. in Zoology at Vijaynagram.

Life at Vijaynagram was dreadful as I had to live in a lodge with other students and eat at a nearby restaurant. I would fall ill often with filaria and would have to then return home to recover. But I ploughed on and finished my B.Sc. I didn't do too well in my exams. The next option available to me was to join the B.Sc. Honours degree. I promptly applied and got into the second year of B.Sc. Honours in Zoology at Andhra University, Vishakhapatnam. All through my early years, my health was a big concern as I was underweight and prone to falling ill. While I was at the University, my health improved considerably but I continued to remain thin.

Andhra University proved to be a turning point in my life because it was there that I realized I had a talent for academics. Given the tough competition and intensive studies, completing the course was proving to be a challenge. But I took it up. The exam was difficult. We were tested in six subjects, with 600 marks for theory and 400 for practical, totalling to 1000 marks. All the exams, comprising the four-year syllabus, had to be finished between Monday and Saturday, without any breaks. It was a nightmare!

Nurturing Influences

At Andhra University, I met a wonderful teacher—Dr. K. Hanumantha Rao, a parasitologist and a guide to Ph.D. students. He taught us invertebrate and vertebrate embryology. His style of teaching made everything more interesting. He made us think harder and be more engaged with the subject. He once showed us a 3D picture of cells bifurcating at the early stages of the egg, which I thought was fascinating! He left a lasting impression on me. And I wanted to be just like him.

After finishing my B.Sc. Honours, I decided to pursue an M.Sc. in Zoology. Naturally, I selected parasitology as my subject for specialization. When the results of B.Sc. Honours were declared, I was pleasantly surprised to find that I had passed with a first class, and had ranked second in the University, with only a two-mark difference between me and the first rank holder.

This was a great achievement for me. I had proven to myself that I could do so much better than what I thought I could. Also, I had surpassed all those students who I thought were 'scholars'. This created a totally different atmosphere at the University for me and gave me a much-needed morale boost.

After B.Sc. Honours, I joined a one-year M.Sc. course with parasitology as a special subject at the same University. Retrospectively, I feel that anybody who could successfully complete B.Sc. Honours from Andhra University at that time can achieve anything in his life. I am one such example. That's the kind of standards that Andhra University maintained in those days.

Dealing with Disappointment

I did well in M.Sc., but to my dismay, my final results were tampered with. I knew who had done it! They had viciously robbed me of my first credit. They altered my original marks and gave me fake rankings. I felt hurt and bitter about it, but I couldn't raise a complaint against the perpetrators. So, I kept my mouth shut. I wanted to do my Ph.D., but I swore I would never do it at Andhra University.

After stepping out of the University, I applied for a job and got appointed as a demonstrator in Zoology at Government Arts College, Rajahmundry, my alma mater. All through my growing up years, my brothers had taken care of my education. They had looked after me and mentored me well. I thought it was time for me to start earning.

Some of my classmates at school were still studying at the College then. I was young and fresh out of the University and brimming with enthusiasm to teach. I took their classes, tutored them, and taught them everything I knew about Zoology. But somehow, they weren't that interested in learning. They were receptive, but not up to my expectations. That led me to feel disillusioned with the teaching profession. Perhaps it was a hasty conclusion. At the age of twenty-one, I was ambitious and full of ideas, but didn't have the patience to carry on due to the lacklustre response of my students.

So, I started looking for other jobs. One day, I came across an advertisement for the position of a research assistant at the Central Institute of Fisheries Technologies. The designation of a research assistant with a central government department sounded nice! I applied for it and got selected on a temporary basis. I had to move from Rajahmundry to Kakinada for this job.

The research assistant post was in the gear and craft of the Fisheries department. Part of the job involved going out in a fishing boat to collect scientific data about various fishing nets such as at what depth the nets were laid down, what was the right time for trawling and what were the different species of fish and prawns in the catch. All this data had to be analyzed to understand the effectiveness of various fishing crafts and gears.

It all sounded very interesting but after working for almost a year, I realized that not much research was actually being done. And I could not imagine a future for myself either in that department or in that research. That's when I made up my mind to return to my original plan—Ph.D. in Zoology.

But where would I study? I had already decided that I would never again study at Andhra University, but I wasn't sure where else to apply. A good friend from the University, Chavali Rama Somayajulu, had gone abroad for higher studies the previous year. His family was from Kakinada and he was attending the Memorial University of Newfoundland at St. John's, Canada. He told me about the department of Biology at his University, and gave me the name of Professor Dr. William Threlfall, in charge of parasitology.

On Somayajulu's advice, I wrote to Prof. William Threlfall expressing my interest in learning under him. Immediately, a letter of acceptance came back. They even agreed to give me a scholarship with the tuition fees waived. All this meant a great deal to me as I didn't have enough savings back then. I detested the idea of being a financial burden on my brothers. Thankfully,

I didn't have to be. My brothers, of course, bought me a one-way ticket and a bag of clothes for my first trip abroad.

Canada Calling

As soon as my admission at the Memorial University was confirmed, I submitted my resignation from the post of temporary research assistant with the central government department. They replied saying they could not relieve me as I had not applied for higher studies through proper channels. Since I couldn't care less, I quit as planned. On 27 September 1967, I set off for Canada.

And that brings me to my most adventurous journey. My flight to St. John's had a stopover at Gander. The plane landed at Gander at midnight but could not continue to its next destination because of the fog. I remember peering outside the airport to find a thick cloak of fog all around, affecting visibility even at two feet. The authorities provided the passengers a bus service to transport us to St. John's. A couple of students from the University had come down to receive me and with them I reached the dormitory at five in the morning. St. John's turned out to be a quaint place in the province of Newfoundland in Canada.

I met Somayajulu once I reached the University. While I was happy to meet my friend, I was happier still to meet Dr. William Threlfall, Supervisor in Parasitology. He was a nice, warm person, and I was excited to work with him for the next two years. He was friendly and guided me throughout my stay at St. John's. It was a refreshing change from the Indian system and I was quite comfortable with their education system. I had to do an M.Sc. in Biology first before applying for a Ph.D. And for my M.Sc. thesis topic, I chose fish parasites in Newfoundland, particularly a marine fish called Cunners, which is a species found in abundance around the province's coast.

Life in Canada was completely different. But since I was used to living in dormitories, I managed well and made some good friends, too. Throughout my stay there I never felt homesick or out of place. Sure, there were plenty of differences in cultures, habits, food and behaviour, but none of these made me feel uneasy because I was focused on my goal—a Ph.D. degree from Canada. The only thing I had trouble with was food—I found Canadian food bland and unpalatable. So, I used to survive on fruit juices, milk and ice creams.

The weather was damp and cold in September. But that didn't bother me because the residences were warm and all the buildings were interconnected with tunnels. While walking from my room to the dining hall or from the laboratory to the library through the tunnels, it hardly mattered that I was in Canada, not India. Late at night I would return from the library hungry. Then I'd buy myself my favourite 'Oh Henry' chocolate for 10 cents from the vending machine. This was my routine almost every day.

What made every inconvenience insignificant was the friendliness of the people there. Our department was like a close-knit family, and everyone made me feel at home. In a way, this helped me excel at my work. Before leaving India, I hadn't done any research about Canada. I only remember reading in my school books that it is famous for fog, cod fish and igloos where the native Indians lived.

After a few months, I met some Indian and Pakistani students on campus and began hanging out with them at the hostel. We spent Sunday evenings watching TV in the common lounge. I remember hurrying through dinner to watch the popular show *Star Trek* every Sunday.

As most of us Indians had the same problem with the hostel food, we decided to cook at the catering facility in the residence. Some nights, we would gather there to cook spicy food to satisfy our taste buds. In those days, very few Indian spices were available in Canada, and even fewer in St. John's. Some of the Indian families we knew got Indian groceries via parcels from New York!

The following summer, my friends and I went sightseeing and discovered that Canadians outside our campus were warm and friendly, too. On Christmas day, Dr. Threlfall invited me to his house for dinner. There I met his wife and three little daughters. As the overseas students lived away from their families, it was the Threlfalls' tradition to invite all the students home for Christmas dinner. They even had a gift for me under the Christmas tree. I can never forget their kindness. Today, I try to look after the boys and girls staying at the hostel at Sankurathri Foundation in the same way so that they don't feel homesick.

Overcoming Barriers

In the initial days, I used to feel a bit uncomfortable because the Canadians couldn't understand my Indian-accented English. But my supervisor often complimented me on my writing skills and wondered how I could write so well in English. Such a compliment, coming from a person of British origin, meant a lot to me and gave a fillip to my confidence. When I had conversations with other students, from Hong Kong and Taiwan, I realized that their accent was completely different. This led me to conclude that even though all of us have learnt English, each one of us has a unique accent and there's no reason for us to feel inferior because of that.

During my second year, a few of my Canadian friends and I decided to learn Russian. To my surprise, they faced problems with Russian pronunciations while it was easier for me to pick up the nuances. Soon, I realized that it was knowing Telugu that helped me with Russian!

It's interesting how my interactions with Canadians helped me understand Indian culture better. During our long discussions, the Indian students used to clear certain misconceptions that Canadians had about Indian culture, which in turn created more awareness among us. I used to actively participate in the Indo–Canada Friendship Association. Since St. John's was a small place and had very few Indians and Pakistanis, and all of them gathered together for functions like a family. I appreciate the simplicity of those days—no bitterness or ill feelings towards each other's communities.

I had come to Canada with a student's visa that allowed me to stay in the country as long as I had admission to a University, with proper financial support. When I was in the second year, my seniors, including those from India, started applying for Canadian immigration. I asked them why. They told me the Canadian government was changing the rules for scholarship eligibility, especially for National Research Council Scholarships. The new rule would mean that only Canadian citizens or landed immigrants were eligible for scholarships. So, I decided to apply for a Canadian Landed Immigrant status, too.

When I went to the Immigration office for an interview, I was asked all kinds of details about my stay in Canada and my education. My initial purpose of coming to Canada was to earn a Ph.D. degree and then go back to India. Quite naively, I informed the Immigration officer of my intentions. He explained to me how immigration is meant for people who want to stay back and work in Canada. I honestly confessed to him that the sole reason I was applying for the Landed Immigration status was to be eligible for a scholarship. With that, my interview concluded. At that time, the Canadian immigration rule was based on a sum total of points. Although I had enough points for them to grant me immigration, I wasn't sure they would give it to me after my performance at the interview. But, luckily, I was granted the Landed Immigration status and I got my papers, which allowed me to stay in Canada for as long as I wanted to, both for studies and work.

Pursuing My Ambition

By April 1969, I finished my research, analyzed my data, completed my experiments and started writing my thesis. And from January 1969 onward I started applying for a Ph.D. in Zoology at various universities, as Memorial University did not offer Ph.D. in Biology. Moreover, I felt that it was a relatively small place and since I had done my Masters there, it was better to move to another University for my Ph.D.

I discussed all this with Dr. Threlfall and he agreed with my point of view. He also helped me with my applications. I had applied to a couple of places both in Canada and the US. Finally, I gained admission with fellowship at the University of Nebraska, USA, and at the University of Alberta, Edmonton, Canada. I wanted to go to Nebraska, but I was not impressed with the research and style of working of the supervisor there.

The supervisor at the University of Alberta, Dr. John C. Holmes, was doing pioneering research in parasite ecology at that time. From 1967 onwards, the study of parasitology was very exciting. Several path-breaking innovations had taken place and new concepts had recently been introduced. And parasite ecology was one of the most promising branches of parasitology.

So, after consulting Dr. Threlfall, I accepted the offer from the University of Alberta. And after finishing my M.Sc. thesis and viva, I packed my bags for Edmonton. Unfortunately, the story of my arrival at St. John's repeated itself. All flights were cancelled due to heavy fog. I managed to reach Edmonton a day or two after I was meant to arrive there. And thus, a new chapter in my Canadian journey began.

Alberta turned out to be much bigger than St. John's. There were more faculty members, and the food was also a lot better; or maybe I was just used to Western food by then.

Taking Change in My Stride

But at Edmonton, the situation was different for me. Dr. Holmes was a great scientist, bright and sharp, but he was completely different from Dr. Threlfall. He wanted his students to be independent. He would never tell us what to do. He used to say that we should tell him what we want to do. I found this very difficult initially, but with time I understood why he was pushing us like that. He wanted to challenge our minds.

To do this, he quizzed us on many things and he gave us opportunities to think on our own and to arrive at our own conclusions.

He taught us a course called Recent Advance in Parasitology, which was held once a week. In that class, we were given a three–four page long reading list that included several journals and textbooks.

Dr. Holmes (at the end of the lecture): Okay, read all those things and come back next week. We will discuss it then.

Me (with a worried expression): So many papers and books, journals and textbooks! How can anybody read all that in a week's time?

Dr. Holmes (smiles): Oh, there is a way to do it. You should learn to read quickly, to analyze the genuineness or usefulness of the printed text. There are techniques that you can use to read and comprehend quickly. All you need to do is master them.

That's the kind of experience he gave me. His technique is the reason why I can read at least three newspapers completely within thirty minutes. The things I learned from Dr. Holmes have remained with me till today.

I managed to finish five years of work in four, including all the field work, lab work and analysis. Every night, I stayed back in the department till nine or ten, sometimes even later. I spent every weekend in the lab or doing field work. I took no breaks or holidays. I didn't mind the hard work because I enjoyed what I was doing. Finally, I finished collecting all the data, wrote the thesis and submitted it to my professor. That was in December 1974. Knowing that Dr. Holmes would take a long time to revert with his feedback, I decided to travel to India.

After seven long years, I returned to my homeland. There had been occasional bouts of homesickness but I used my work as a shield and kept loneliness at bay. Now with my thesis done and my Ph.D. goal almost achieved, I allowed myself to be swayed by the love of my country, my family and my friends. I was back home and my happiness was complete.

On that trip, I met many people in India. And all of them discouraged me from settling down in India. A bit confused, I went back to Canada wondering what the future held for me.

A Home of My Own

The centre table was filled with goodies, but I didn't feel like eating anything. I had lost my appetite because of the embarrassment. There were at least a dozen people in the room, most of them strangers, all staring at me expectantly. They asked me a few insane questions and I found it difficult to make my answers audible. 'This is worse than a job interview,' I muttered. Yes, you guessed it—I was here to meet my prospective bride.

My first visit to India in 1974 involved meeting family and friends, and a couple of failed attempts at 'choosing a bride'. As I had almost completed my Ph.D., my relatives thought that it was high time I got married. They arranged for a few girls to be 'shown' to me. Although I was not averse to the idea of arranged marriage, I didn't find the girls I met interesting at all. So, I flew back to Canada in January 1975, without tying the knot, much to everyone's disappointment.

Coming back home after seven years was an eye-opener. Life in Canada had changed me. The crowds and the general lack of order when I reached Delhi airport made me claustrophobic. Even my conversations with acquaintances often led to embarrassing silences as I was unable to connect with people other than my family.

But what affected me the most was the poverty and filth that I saw everywhere. I used to wonder 'Why is my country like this? Why can't it be clean, like Canada?' I wanted to do something that would make a difference but didn't know what or how.

Going back to India also reinforced the difference in education standards of the two countries. I had gone to St. John's armed with a Master's degree in Zoology. However, over there, I was forced to again take admission for an M.Sc. degree in Biology. Initially I was reluctant, but while studying for the course I realized that the M.Sc. degrees in India and Canada were completely different from each other. Studying for a Master's degree in Canada helped me understand the deficiencies in my education and academic foundation, as well as in English.

The two years that I spent at St. John's convinced me that another M.Sc. course had not been a waste of time. It had made me a better student. I did well while pursuing my Ph.D. at Alberta University and hardly faced any problem in completing my studies.

My Career Path

On my way back from India, I made a two-day stopover at my childhood friend Raju's home in the UK. An ophthalmologist by profession, Raju had settled in the UK with his wife, Rani. After a fun couple of days, I was preparing to catch my flight to Canada from Gatwick airport, London. Before I left, we felt that we should take a picture of the three of us together. Raju suggested that the landing outside the front door was a good place for the photograph and ushered us outside. Unwittingly, he shut the door behind him.

Rani screamed, 'I don't have the keys with me!' My luggage was inside the house and it was almost time for me to leave for the airport. Raju quickly drove over to the landlady's house and got spare keys from her. I took my luggage and hurried to the airport. As I was late to check in, they asked me to carry my luggage onto the airplane. I am sure I made a funny sight, running to the boarding gate with all my bags. Surprisingly, they accommodated me in business class. To this day, that flight remains one of the most memorable incidents of my life.

In 1974, the government of Canada had made Canadian citizenship mandatory for those looking for jobs in the country, with employment preference given to Canadian citizens over landed immigrants. On my return to Canada, I applied for citizenship and got it without any hassle.

My guide got back to me with feedback on my thesis and after examining my final work, the University awarded me with a Ph.D. degree in parasitology in September 1974. Armed with a doctorate degree and Canadian citizenship, I started applying for jobs and scholarships. In October 1974, I bagged the postdoctoral National

Research Council Fellowship (NRC) to continue my work at a prestigious research station in fisheries, which was under the Fisheries and Oceans Department. Its laboratory was called Pacific Biological Station, and pioneering research in all fields of fisheries, including fish parasitology, was conducted there.

I had to move to Nanaimo in British Columbia for this fellowship. There I met two top-notch research scientists in parasitology—Dr. Z. Kabata and Dr. Leo Margolis. Dr. Kabata was my immediate supervisor while Dr. Margolis was the head of Parasitology at the Pacific Biological Station. I learnt a lot from both of them and that learning shaped my personality.

Dr. Kabata had run away from his home country, Poland, during the Second World War. He was only seventeen then. He used to narrate stories about his struggle, which were awe-inspiring. He was a meticulous person, highly disciplined and punctual. Apart from his contributions to Parasitology, he was also an artist. During my association with him, I discovered a new genus and species of a Microsporidian parasite located in the kidney of a sea fish called Hake in the Pacific Ocean.

Dr. Margolis was also a fish parasitologist, but his specialty was the study of round worms living in the salmon fish of the Pacific Ocean. His study proved to be a breakthrough in identifying the stocks of salmon fish in the Pacific based on the presence of these round worms. He was also an efficient administrator and a compassionate person. Working under him was an enriching experience for me.

Marriage on the Cards

I had scheduled my second visit to India in the summer of 1975. I felt that I was ready for marriage and I asked my family to do a preliminary screening of the girls. I was uncomfortable with the idea of meeting too many of them. I also had a condition—I should be allowed to speak to the girl directly. It was not a common custom at that time.

My family had shortlisted four girls. The first one was Manjari. The minute I saw her, I knew she was the one. I flatly refused to meet the other three girls. I had made up my mind to marry Manjari. During the meeting, I asked her a few questions about her studies and life.

Usually, the boy has to go over to the girl's place to meet her. But since I didn't have too many holidays, my brother arranged for Manjari and her family to come over to Hyderabad. She was put up at her brother, Dr. C. V. Ram Mohan's place. As soon as I announced my decision to marry Manjari, I requested our respective families to arrange the wedding before I returned to Canada.

This wasn't a problem because we had very few

relatives. But Manjari's two elder sisters were holidaying. They had to cut short their holiday to attend the wedding. I knew I had caused inconveniences to too many people. Later, Manjari would often remind me how I had thrown tradition out of the window and hurried everyone. I would smile and reply, 'It's your fault. Why didn't you meet me sooner?'

I got married to Manjari on 12 May 1975, in her hometown, Kakinada, in peak Indian summer. On our wedding day, it was exceptionally hot. The reception took place the following day in Hyderabad. Within a few days of the wedding, I left for Canada. I didn't get a chance to mingle well with Manjari's family, but I realized early on that they were all well-educated, simple and affectionate people.

After reaching Nanaimo, I sent all relevant papers to Manjari to process her immigration. I couldn't wait for her to come live with me! Since the wedding happened in such a rush, I had barely had the chance to get to know her. But later, we used to write letters to each other to make up for being so far apart. 'Dear Chandra' and 'Dear Manju' became our most eagerly awaited words.

Adjusting to a New Life

Manju landed in Vancouver in the October of 1975. We travelled to Nanaimo and started building our life together.

Manju was supportive in many ways. To begin with, she never complained about adjusting to a new country and lifestyle. Even though she was typically Indian, she had no qualms about staying in Canada. Friendly and warm by nature and fluent in English, she would mix easily with our neighbours. She was a woman of patience, perseverance and understanding. Even if she did have problems adjusting to Canada, she never expressed them to me. But I knew that she missed India and her family terribly. She would anxiously wait for letters from India, and sometimes used to make calls to her family.

Manju took up a job as a research assistant at the laboratory where I was working. Although she wasn't ambitious, she enjoyed her stint at the lab. And she was able to easily manage our home and her work. I helped her around the house as much as I could, but she preferred doing household work on her own.

Moving Ahead

For a parasitologist, there were few job options available then. When I got an offer from the Department of Wildlife, Ottawa, I knew this was the closest I could get to an academic research job. So, I accepted it and moved to Ottawa in the midst of a snowstorm on 7 January 1977.

After two years of living in pleasant British Columbia,

the snowstorms of Ottawa came as a shock. Manju had to set up a home all over again and leave her job. Yet, she did not once complain. She always chose to see the silver lining in every situation. She disliked the bulky winter clothing, but she loved playing in the snow. At home, she would spend her free time knitting, sewing and embroidering, or practising her music, or gardening. Her happy and cheerful disposition filled the house with positivity.

Our first friends in Ottawa were Dr. Sarma Vishnubhatla and his wife Lakshmi. They showed us various apartments and helped us settle into a house close to their place. We met them in 1977 and our bond of friendship remains strong till date. The good doctor and his wife supported us in a new place and that's something I shall never forget.

Before marriage, Manju had completed the first year of a two-year diploma in Carnatic music at Madras Music College. She had to give this up when she moved to Canada, a regret she shared with me.

Manju: I wish I had finished my diploma course in Carnatic music. I missed out on being a better singer.

Me: No, my dear, that's not true. You are a wonderful singer and I haven't seen such voice modulation even in professional singers. Anyway, you had great teachers—your sisters. No formal training could have matched that.

Manju would smile at this and momentarily lose herself in memories of her sisters and their music.

Apart from her three musical sisters, Manju had four brothers. Her father was a retired police officer. Theirs was a warm, affectionate family. I consider myself lucky to have married into their family and luckier still to have had a wife like Manju. I feel that the ten years of our marriage taught me a great deal. She has enriched my life in more ways than one, my two wonderful children being the best gift of all.

Our life in Ottawa was different from Nanaimo. We made a lot of friends from the Telugu community there. My job was interesting, and our married life was filled with joy because Manju was expecting. But soon, things took a turn for the worse—at the end of 1977, Manju had a miscarriage.

She took it badly and her sadness showed on her health and mood. I thought it better to take her to India to quicken her recovery. So, around February 1978, we returned home. I went back to Canada in a month's time, while Manju stayed in India for another month or two.

With family by her side, Manju was returning to her normal self again. By the time she was to return to Canada, she was jubilant. During her stay in Kakinada, she had discovered that she was pregnant again.

A new chapter in our lives was about to begin, and we got busy preparing for parenthood.

chapter three

The Wonder Years

18 November 1978
Riverside Hospital, Ottawa

Doctor: Any complaints?

Me: None, doctor. I've just brought her for her weekly check-up.

Doctor: Her reports are absolutely fine. The baby is healthy and we expect him to come by mid-December. So, relax! There's no cause for worry.

Manju: Thank you, doctor.

Doctor: I will be on leave for the next ten days. But I will be back well in time for the delivery. Now go home and take rest.

After that reassuring conversation with the gynaecologist, we headed home where Manju's parents were eagerly waiting for us. They came to visit us in Ottawa during the summer and stayed back to be with their daughter during her first pregnancy. They were delighted to hear of the good progress both mother and baby were making. The next two days remained uneventful. However, early in the morning on the 20th, Manju went into labour. We rushed her to the hospital and within two hours she delivered a healthy baby boy. The doctor's assurance that the baby was healthy proved to be true, but our son totally disregarded his prediction and arrived weeks ahead of the due date.

Since he was premature, the hospital authorities suspected that he might be under-developed and thought it best to keep him in an incubator. The paediatrician in-charge was happy with the initial examination, which concluded that although the baby was small, his bodily functions were fine. He was active and suckling properly.

Relief swept over us. My son was finally here, and he shared my birthday!

Raising Srikiran

Once Manju and the baby were home, everything was completely different. There were relatives milling around us and everyone fussed over the new mother. The happiness we felt on holding the baby and answering his demands was indescribable.

There was a huge family debate about what name

to give the baby. Manju's brothers, sisters, nieces and nephews all offered their suggestions. There was one particular nephew of hers, called Sricharan, who wanted the baby's name to be similar to his. Manju and I thought the name Kiran was apt for the baby, as he was born at dawn. So, we clubbed the two names together and decided to name him Srikiran. He was a great favourite with his uncles, aunts and cousins. And he loved them back in equal measure.

Raising Srikiran was a beautiful experience. He was our bundle of joy and we were completely preoccupied with him. A lovely and smiling child, he never caused us any trouble. Even as a toddler, he had a friendly and outgoing nature. Once, when the three of us were at a restaurant, a young couple at the next table was playing with eighteen-month old Srikiran. The young man then turned to me and said, 'You have a charming boy. He will have lots of girls flocking around him when he grows up!' We had a hearty laugh at this.

One day, while waiting in the queue to pay the bill at the supermarket, Srikiran noticed a matchbox car and demanded to have it. We shushed him and Manju told him he could have it later. He agreed and we walked out of the store. A young man who had been standing behind us in the queue hurriedly came up to us and gave Srikiran the car. He was thrilled. That night he slept with the car under his pillow. This continued for many years.

And that blue matchbox car was the beginning of his passion for cars.

Soon, he started collecting toy cars. His first drawing was also that of a car. He was so good at identifying cars that he could name the brand and model of any passing car. I used to wonder how he got to know so much about cars.

Bright and well-behaved, Srikiran was a fast learner and a sensitive child. Uncomplaining, like his mother, he was always on the lookout for something to do. By the time he was two, he was in and out of activities such as drawing, painting and paper cutting. He also had an aptitude for music. He enjoyed listening to it and we took delight in watching him shake his head to the rhythm. Although he never sat down with his mother to learn music, he was familiar with Carnatic music and appreciated it in his own way. Every night Manju would sing a lullaby—the *Kheera Sagara Vihara*—to him. Without that particular lullaby in his mother's sweet voice, there was no sleep for Srikiran.

He was an early riser and would be up every day at the crack of dawn with a smile on his lips. I remember watching cartoons with him on TV every Saturday. He wasn't much into TV but Saturday mornings were devoted to father–son cartoon watching.

Manju inculcated the habit of reading in Srikiran. We had a set of sixteen books of stories on how to be a good person; Manju would repeatedly read these books to Srikiran.

Our neighbourhood had many condominiums like ours as well as town houses. Across our house was a park, which was a favourite with Srikiran. His mother used to take him there to play with other children. Apart from a stray incident of mischief when he had pulled a little girl's hair, there were no complaints about him. He was a good playmate for the neighbourhood kids.

Manju would also speak to him a lot about India and about our relatives there. So, Srikiran ended up knowing everyone back in India by their names. When he started asking about them, we would record his voice and send the recordings to our family members in India. Manju's brother and sister would come over during the holidays, and their kids would sometimes stay over for two–three weeks. Srikiran would have a great time at home with his cousins.

When he was around four, we began taking him for piano lessons. A high school student named Mareek used to teach Srikiran piano after school.

Srikiran picked it up as if he was born to play it. He finished two books in a span of three months. All of us were surprised by this. I couldn't afford to buy him a piano and his music lessons were temporarily stalled. I often wonder how proficient a piano player he would have turned out to be had he been alive today.

Apart from music, there was another thing that caught his interest at the tender age of five—science. I had bought him a few children's science books, which were full of information about dinosaurs, planets, the animal kingdom and space. That's how he discovered his interest in astronomy. Instead of bedtime stories, he asked me to read out from the science books. He kept bombarding me with questions as I read. I answered them as precisely as I could but you can't answer all the questions a five-year-old asks, especially one as smart as Srikiran. I had to gently scold him, and make him shut his eyes. As soon as I closed the book, he would fall asleep. His inquisitive mind would be lost in vivid dreams that his active imagination conjured up, only to wake up with more questions about the world around him. Listening to him talk, I often wondered how such a young mind could be so curious. It was his best quality and I always tried to satisfy his curiosity.

As a toddler, Srikiran was a fussy eater. Feeding Srikiran was a big chore as he never used to co-operate. But all that changed when Sarada was born.

It's a Girl!

When Srikiran was one-and-a-half, we started planning our second child. Manju's second pregnancy was a protracted one. She had to visit the gynaecologist several times during the term. Even her labour was long and difficult. Finally, Sarada—a happy, beautiful baby girl—was born on 17 July 1981.

Srikiran got along very well with the newest member of our family; no sibling rivalry whatsoever. He quickly became her protective elder brother. His first encounter with his baby sister set the tone of his behaviour. Manju delivered Sarada at Ottawa Civic Hospital and I brought Srikiran along to meet his mother. Instead of rushing to meet Manju, he headed first to the crib to see Sarada. 'He doesn't even want to talk to me anymore!' Manju exclaimed.

Soon after Sarada was born, Manju's sister, Dr. Sitalakshmi Nunna, came over to help her. One day, we were all sitting in the living room and talking about the possible names for Sarada. While our discussion was on, Srikiran was busy with his Lego set. Several names were mentioned in the course of our conversation. Suddenly, Srikiran turned around and announced, 'I like Sarada (he pronounced it "Dada").' Dr. Sitalakshmi said she doesn't like Sarada but prefers Ambujakshi. But Srikiran was adamant. He insisted that Sarada was better than all the other names, certainly better than Ambujakshi. We were surprised at his reaction, especially since he was all of two-and-a-half years old and unable even to pronounce the name properly. Finally, we decided to go with his choice and named our baby girl Sarada.

My little girl was completely different from her older brother. She was like a Russian doll—a doll within another. In front of outsiders, Sarada was shy and introverted. But with family members, she was forthcoming and playful.

Whenever she came across a stranger, she would hide behind me or Manjari and observe everyone quietly. Even when we had guests over, she would not socialize with them while Srikiran befriended everyone. But as soon as the guests left, Sarada would recount everything that happened. Her personality was different. Every evening she used to come out of the house to receive me and carry my briefcase inside, chattering about her day throughout. It was fun to watch her struggling to carry the briefcase that was clearly too heavy for her.

Although Manju took her to the park, she had few friends there. Her real friends were her mother and brother, both of whom she adored. Like them, she was musically inclined and a bookworm. Once she accompanied them to an event in which both Manju and Srikiran were participating. She quietly observed everyone during the performance. When we returned, she re-enacted the entire performance. We were surprised by her acting skills. That's when we realized that behind the quiet facade was a keen and observant mind.

She differed from her brother on many counts. She was not as physically active as Srikiran, preferred sitting still to prancing around. And she was surprisingly impatient. As a toddler, she would quickly complete her drawings while Srikiran would work meticulously. While Srikiran would be up at 5 a.m., Sarada needed warm-up sessions before she got out of bed by 7.

She was fond of chatting with her brother. So, every day after he returned from school, both the siblings would sit together and chat. Srikiran regaled her with stories about school. His stories appealed to her and she longed to go to school. In Canada, schooling started with kindergarten. There was no concept of lower kindergarten, like we have in India. Since Sarada was only three, it was too early for her to start school. To keep her happy, we bought her a small school bag. Every morning she would dress up, put on her school bag and announce to everyone that she was going to 'cool'. Young as she was, she couldn't even pronounce school. But nothing mattered to her, and the whole house would be filled with her exuberant voice chanting 'I'm going to "cool", I'm going to "cool"!

Her wish of going to school remained unfulfilled. When I returned to Kakinada and started the school, I named it Sarada Vidyalayam in the memory of my little girl and her unfulfilled dream. When I see hundreds of children go to the school that's named after her, I feel a great sense of satisfaction.

Experiencing Parenthood

Parenting was an enriching experience for us. Manju was always fond of children. She completely dedicated herself to raising them. Since Srikiran was our firstborn, we had many anxious moments with him. Any sound from his room and Manju would rush to check on him. As an infant, Srikiran slept on his stomach, which caused her to fret about his breathing. With Sarada, she constantly worried about her weight as she was thin. The paediatrician called her a 'worry worm' and asked her not to bother about the weight as long as Sarada was healthy and active. Raising Srikiran and Sarada was a continuous learning process. But since Manju is inherently calm and patient, she made it look effortless.

We were very focused on one aspect—making sure our kids were rooted in our culture. Both the children called their mother 'Amma' and addressed me as 'Nanna'. We taught Sarada to call Srikiran 'Anna' ('brother', in Telugu). We made sure that we spoke in Telugu at home so that both the kids were familiar with their mother tongue. And we inculcated Indian values and habits as much as possible.

The Householder's Life

My everyday life in Canada was like any other. I preferred going to work early to avoid rush-hour traffic, so, I used to be out of bed by 5.30 every morning. After a light breakfast of cereal with banana and milk, I would take the peanut-butter-jelly sandwiches, which Manju packed for my lunch, and be off to work by 7 a.m. I worked till 3 p.m. and reached home by 3.30 every afternoon. As soon as I parked my car, Sarada would be at my side to welcome me home. Sometimes I would stop by at the departmental store to buy supplies. However, weekends were reserved for shopping expeditions with my wife and kids.

My working hours allowed me to spend quality time with my children. After I left for work, Manju would send Srikiran to school. He, too, carried PBJ sandwiches for lunch. He would be back home around the same time as I. We had dinner around 5.30 or 6 in the evening and spent time before bed by playing, talking or teaching the kids.

Manju's relatives who were settled in the US, such as her eldest sister Dr. Sitalakshmi, her husband and her four daughters, often visited us from their home in Pittsburgh. Her brother, C. Ramakrishna, lived in New Jersey with his wife Vijaya and a daughter and son, while her younger brother, Durga Prasad, lived in Allentown, Pennsylvania. My sister-in-law, Kausalya, and my brother, Venkat Rao, also called on us frequently. On my side of the family, my elder brothers, Dr. Rau and Mr. S. V. B. Rao, who was an Air India employee, paid us regular visits.

I had applied for US green cards for all four of us, and in 1981 we got them. However, Manju wasn't keen on moving as she had become comfortable in Canada.

An Exceptional Woman

With two kids to raise, Manju had her hands full. When she first came to Canada, she had taken up the job of research assistant at the same lab where I was working in Nanaimo. However, after the children were born, she decided to take a break from work until both of them began school. Since Sarada was still a baby, it wouldn't have been possible for my wife to start working for another four–five years.

She was a good singer and practised regularly at home. Sometimes, I asked her to sing for me. At every social function, especially if it was organized by the South Indian Cultural Association, she was requested to sing. Manju, however, lacked confidence and thought her singing was not up to the mark. I would do my best to boost her morale and persuade her to sing. And everyone would love her performance.

In spite of all the praise and applause she received, she remained a humble and simple person. She never demanded expensive clothes or jewellery. Instead, she looked for ways to be helpful to the needy. If she came across a poor family, she made it a point to talk to them, and help them in whichever way she could.

Looking back, I appreciate empathy, but at the time I felt we were not that well off that we should be thinking of bettering other people's lives. I would sometimes tell her we should not look at those less fortunate than us, but focus on improving our lives. She would smile serenely at me and do what she wanted to do. I have tried to imbibe Manju's virtues over the years.

Manju had a very unique way of judging people. Once, she told me, 'If a person is fond of plants or gardening, then he will be kind-hearted.' Now with experience, I know this to be true. I feel her sixth sense has rubbed off on me, too. Every time I meet a new person, I feel certain vibes. It has helped me a lot while dealing with people, especially while hiring them. I try not to be judgemental but trust my intuition in assessing the person's calibre.

Our friends and neighbours thought of us as an ideal couple. We had few arguments. We believed in sharing each other's burdens and joys. I helped her with household chores after coming back from office as I knew it was exhausting to look after two kids. Whenever Manju went shopping, she bought things for me, for the children and for the house, never anything for herself. So, I ended up shopping for her. Other women from our community often enviously remarked, 'Look how lucky Manju is—her husband shops for her.' Little did they know that it was I who was lucky to have a wife like her. Such was the harmony of our domestic life that my father-in-law, who visited us once, went back to India and told his other children that Manju and I were living in Canada 'like a pair of Juno swans'.

In December 1984, Manju dreamt that the Sarmas had moved into a new house, far away from us. She had a special gift of premonition and was often right in her predictions.

When we met the Sarmas on New Year's Eve, she casually asked them if they were planning to shift houses. They denied it. However, in April 1985, they called to inform us that they were moving into their new home near the airport. We were, of course, surprised.

After settling into their new place, they invited us over. The area was completely new to me, so I took down instructions from Dr. Sarma before driving there with Manju and the kids. During the drive, she kept pointing out the directions to me. She knew which turns I had to take. And as soon as the house came into view, she pointed it out to me. 'That's the one—that's Dr. Sarma's new house. It is the one I saw in my dream.'

Later that year, we heard about the tumult in India over Operation Blue Star and the firing inside Amritsar's Golden Temple. After we saw the news, Manju had another dream, and she told me all about it.

Manjari: I had another dream. It was more of a nightmare, actually.

Me: What was it about?

Manjari: I saw that all four of us had gone to attend a big social function. We were eating and enjoying ourselves when suddenly a group of sardarjis thronged the place with machine guns in their hands. They opened fire. Everyone started screaming and running for their lives.

Me: Where was I?

Manjari: I don't know. I looked around for you but you were nowhere to be seen. It was just me, Srikiran and Sarada facing the sardarjis' bullets.

Me: In that case, it's not likely to happen. You never go anywhere without me. Since the news of Operation Blue Star and Mrs. Gandhi's assassination and riots in Delhi are repeatedly going on, you must be thinking about it all the time. All this must have induced that nightmare.

I brushed aside her dream. But her dream keeps coming back to me even today. What she saw in her dream would eventually come true.

Both Srikiran and Sarada, in their unique ways, added immeasurable happiness to our lives. They made our lives complete, they made our family complete, they made us complete. Every little detail about them is etched clearly in my memory, even after thirty years.

Manju was a dedicated mother. When they fell ill, she was up on her feet night and day, nursing them, not sleeping a wink. Sometimes, I used to wonder at how attached she was to them. On that ill-fated flight, she must have held them tight and they must have disappeared like a unit ... I am sure of that. Deep down in my heart I know that Manju and the children are together, wherever they are.

Today, when I see young men and women, I try to visualize how Srikiran and Sarada would have looked. What would they have become? What career paths would they have chosen? When I hear a girl say she was born in 1981, immediately a vision of Sarada, as a young woman, springs before my eyes. Such thoughts spontaneously pass through my mind and I can do nothing to control them. I guess that's how it is meant to be ... that I will watch my children grow up only in my imagination.

chapter four

Turn of the Tide

The morning of 22 June 1985 dawned like any other day. The house was abuzz with activity as Manjari took care of last-minute packing. The kids couldn't control their excitement at the thought of meeting their grandparents, aunts, uncles and cousins. They were going to India.

Sarada was too young to remember her previous trips to India, but Srikiran, who was going on his third trip, had many stories to tell her. This time, we were going to India for the wedding of Manju's youngest brother, Bhavani Prasad. I say 'we' but it was only Manjari and the kids who were leaving for India that day. Since school ended in June, we thought it would be a good idea for them to have a vacation in India. I had to finish some work in Canada, so I was meant to join them in July.

A wedding is always a big affair in Indian households. The four of us were thrilled. It was a double treat for us—a wedding and a visit to India. Manjari had bought gifts for everyone. By evening, everything was set. It was a late-night flight from Montreal. Our neighbour had agreed to drive us to the airport in his station wagon.

When we reached the airport, we were told that the flight was delayed. As we waited patiently, Srikiran decided to make fun of Sarada.

Srikiran: Do you know how high the plane flies? Miles and miles away from the Earth!

Sarada: How exciting!

Srikiran: Don't get too excited, you never know what will happen in mid-air. Our plane might get hijacked.

Sarada: What is hijacked?

Srikiran: Hijacking is when terrorists come with machine guns and take over the plane and make it go wherever they want.

Sarada: What about us?

Srikiran: Oh! They will kidnap us too!

Sarada (looking alarmed): Kidnap! Nanna, see what Anna is saying. He says we are all going to get kidnapped!

Me: Don't pay any attention to him. He is simply pulling your leg. Srikiran, don't scare her like this.

Srikiran was in splits by this time.

Amidst this childish banter, the flight was announced. Manjari proceeded towards the security check area with the children. Waving and laughing, they boarded the aircraft.

Air India Flight 182 was served by Boeing 747-237B, better known as Emperor Kanishka. The flight route was Montreal-London-Delhi. Taking off from Montréal-Mirabel International Airport, Canada, at 12.30 a.m. on 23 June 1985, it was scheduled to stopover at London Heathrow Airport, UK, before reaching its final destination at Indira Gandhi International Airport, New Delhi, India.

After the plane took off, I returned home. Exhausted by the excitement of the day, I instantly feel asleep. Around 6 a.m., the doorbell rang. Still groggy, I reached for the main door and opened it. To my surprise, a group of my friends and neighbours had gathered there. Their faces were grave and they remained silent for what seemed like ages. Too dazed and confused, I merely moved aside to let them in. Slowly, the living room was filled with people. They made me sit down on the sofa. Before I could ask them anything, one of them said, 'The plane has gone off the radar.'

Grappling with the Truth

'Off the radar'—the words ricocheted in my head. What do they mean 'off the radar'? Then they started telling me the news. We turned on the TV to get latest updates.

Flight 182 had reportedly been bombed mid-air. It had crashed in the Atlantic Ocean, off the coast of Cork in Ireland. The news flashed across all channels.

It was touted as a major tragedy, the likes of which Canada had never witnessed. It was undoubtedly a terrorist attack but the perpetrators of the attack were not named. The channels gave details of the travelling passengers—how they were a mix of Canadians and Indians, with a majority being Canadian immigrants of Indian origin. There were 329 passengers on board. There were no survivors.

'No survivors', 'tragedy', 'Kanishka bombing' ... these words kept echoing in the house. But to me they appeared meaningless. It refused to sink in. I drew a complete blank. I didn't know what I was saying, why I was saying it, whom I was talking to, what I was doing. Everything became a blur.

But even in this state of mind, I could somehow continue with my daily routine. I was able to sleep, eat and work normally. My mind refused to believe what had really happened. For the longest time, I lived in denial. I refused to accept that they would never return to me.

My neighbours, friends and colleagues were very sympathetic. They tried to help me in every way. But my communication with them was merely superficial, as I hadn't come to terms with it. My brothers and brothers-in-law came over to comfort me. Manjari's elder brother took me with him to New Jersey. After staying with him for a few days, I returned to Ottawa.

The house seemed eerie. I knew it would feel silent and empty with Manjari and the kids in India, but now the emptiness took on a chilling aspect. It was almost as if the air inside that house was haunted by their memories, their laughter, their voices, their footsteps. Each morning as I sat down for breakfast, I would almost see Manjari walk towards me with my lunchbox. As I left the house, I would almost see Srikiran waving good-bye. And as I returned home, I would almost see Sarada come running towards the car park, demanding to carry my bag for me. Well, almost! I felt them, saw them, heard them ... but they were not there.

The emptiness of the house reinforced the truth. They were gone! With that, a flood of tears would overwhelm me. I would cry for hours on end, especially when I listened to music. It had been such an intrinsic part of our lives—the memories it evoked were so real. But I always kept my grief private, never shedding a tear in public or amidst friends. The word 'difficult' cannot describe the life I led in the months following the accident. It seemed as if I was leading a dual life—one in the outside world where I could talk, eat and work normally, and the other, within which tears and emptiness were my constant companions.

Call for Identification

One day, news came in that the crashed plane had been found off the coast of Cork in Ireland, and some bodies had been discovered. I, along with other families of the victims, was called on to identify the bodies. Remains of 120 people were found. Not all of them were identified, as the bodies were damaged beyond recognition. My brother, Dr. Rau, and Manju's eldest brother, Ramakrishna, accompanied me to Cork to help me deal with this.

I gulped down the bitter nausea in my throat as I read through the list of identified people. My family's names were not in that list. Next, we were taken to the morgue where the bodies were preserved. We were shown a few belongings and asked to identify them. None of the broken or charred things belonged to Manjari or the children. Then we were shown photographs of the mutilated bodies that lay frozen in the recesses of the morgue. There are no words to describe my feelings when I looked at those pictures. As one photo changed to the next, my heart beat faster—half expecting that the next one would be them, half praying for it not to be. Teary-eyed, I forced myself to go through all the photographs.

The extent of the tragedy revealed itself through the photos. I realized that I might have encountered at least a few of these people at the airport on the night I dropped my family there. Happy faces waving cheerful goodbyes ... and now reduced to this! Bits and pieces of charred flesh with nothing but a number identifying and acknowledging their existence.

Manjari, Srikiran and Sarada were not in those pictures. What did it mean for me? Did it mean I could continue with the delusional hope that they were not dead and would come back one day? I did go through a phase of denial when I refused to accept that they were dead—longing, yearning, almost willing them to come back and make complete our broken home. But that phase ended after my visit to Cork. I fully understood and accepted the truth.

However, I was grateful that their bodies were not found. Their memories were intact with me, not marred by images of disfigured bodies. In my mind, Manjari was always smiling her serene, content smile, with Srikiran and Sarada beaming with unaffected happiness and love as they hugged her.

Coming to Terms

From Cork, we travelled to India. Hema akka insisted that we complete their last rites in our hometown. I was quite indifferent to the whole thing. I did as I was told, but my heart was elsewhere. I had reached a point when I knew none of these rituals mattered. A few days later,

I returned to Canada and tried to put back the pieces of my life.

I joined a support group for survivor families. From this group, I remember Dr. Yogesh Paliwal who had lost his second son, and Dr. Anantraman who lost his wife and two daughters in the tragedy. At the meetings, we were asked to share our feelings and experiences, and help each other overcome our grief. However, I ended up giving support to members of that group rather than taking it from them. I recall how inconsolable Dr. Anantraman was—he would not step out of his house, not speak with anybody and spend hours crying. For well over a year, he left everything in his house exactly as it was on the day his family left for India. I did my best to help him come to terms with the tragedy. A few years after coming back to India, I learnt that Dr. Anantraman, too, had quit Canada and shifted to his hometown in Tamil Nadu where he was running a school.

During this time, I befriended a young man called Marc Andre Cote. He joined my office in 1986 and over the next two years, a special friendship fostered between us. Although I was senior to him in years and experience, he became a good friend. I used to counsel and guide him both on professional and personal aspects of life. He still remains in touch with me.

I met a Canadian couple who were running a children's home in Hyderabad. I volunteered to work for them and helped them with fundraising. On one of my trips to

India, I visited the children's home and was appalled by the way it worked. Hema akka had volunteered to teach the children there. She spent considerable time there and was able to give me more feedback on how the home was run. I gave my feedback to the Canadian couple, who did not take it in the right spirit. I sensed their discomfort, and that's when I realized that I should be doing something on my own.

In 1987, Hema akka visited me in Canada. I returned with her to India for a visit. En route, we went to Cork and visited its coast. Once we landed in India, I started planning what I could do for my people.

Soon I made up my mind to quit my job and settle down in India for good.

This decision drew many detractors. Many people tried to persuade me not to give up the comforts of Canada, and come to live in a small town in India. But I was firm. My family, of course, was supportive of this idea. The following year, in 1988, two of my nephews, Narain and Rajendra, came to Canada to help me pack up. In mid-July 1988, I quit Canada and returned to India.

Relocating Life

'Don't go, Chandra! Your life is here. This is your home. This is where Manju and the kids lived. There's nothing for you in India,' my mind kept insisting. My heart, on the other hand, was set to fly back to my homeland. I was piecing together my life without Manju, Srikiran and Sarada, but I knew that it will never be complete.

I couldn't make myself go back to my old way of life. I had reached a fork in the road. And I had to choose a path that would make my life bearable to begin with, and then over time, more fulfilling.

In 1987, I had bought a piece of land outside Kakinada, with the aim of starting an orphanage. I wound up my life in Canada, informed everyone that I was moving back, submitted my resignation to the Federal Government in Ottawa, cashed in my pension and packed my bags. My friends there wondered what I was up to. They tried to dissuade me from taking such a drastic step. But I was determined to return to India.

I was from Rajahmundry and Manju was from Kakinada. It somehow felt 'right' to start my life afresh in the town where my beloved wife grew up. In June 1988, I boarded the return flight to India with expectations, scepticism and uncomfortable feelings as my companions. In spite of my misgivings, I knew that I wanted to work with underprivileged and orphaned children in India.

In Kakinada, I stayed at my in-laws' home. But I didn't want to be a burden on them forever, for they were as grief-stricken as I. So, my first job was to build a house for myself.

However, I soon realized that as an NRI, I couldn't own agricultural land in India. I thought it was an ancient, outdated law, but as I was a law-abiding citizen, I wanted to figure out the right solution to this problem.

I approached the Reserve Bank of India in Mumbai and explained my dilemma. The officers didn't have any solutions for me. Instead, they told me to sell the land and leave the country!

But I had a brainwave! I decided to transfer the land to my sister, Hema akka. She had moved from Hyderabad to Kakinada to be with me. Hema akka had always been supportive towards everyone in the family, generously making sacrifices for her loved ones. Now she was sacrificing her career for my sake.

Today, when I look around my garden, I can't believe I almost lost this land due to some outdated laws. I love sitting on the porch in the morning, and enjoying the beautiful scenery.

As soon as the land was transferred in Hema akka's name, we applied for the permit to build our first home here, so that all the activities of the Foundation could be initiated.

In the meantime, my in-laws and relatives started urging me to remarry. Initially, they dropped hints, referring to the importance of having a family. Then they started bringing me marriage proposals. I couldn't brush them off rudely, so I kept delaying them. However, after meeting a couple of women, I had to tell them to stop.

I was managing on my own because I had a goal to achieve. My work was taking up all my time. But I knew that these weren't the real reasons. The truth was that I knew nobody could take Manju's place in my life, and I saw no point in marrying another woman who I could never love as much as I did Manju. Eventually, my relatives accepted this and dropped the subject of re-marriage.

Building the House

We got permission to start construction in 1989 and immediately started building the house. Before I left Canada, many of my friends promised to visit me in Kakinada. I wanted my new home to accommodate visitors, so I thought of building a five-bedroom house. Each room was to be equipped with an attached bathroom, apart from the kitchen and living room. I always had a fascination for sloping roofs, perhaps because I grew up in a house that had one. I conveyed my ideas to the architect and asked him to create a design for a five-bedroom house. However, I was not pleased with the results. Finally, after changing seven architects, I zeroed in on the architect whose design was up to my expectations.

During this time, I also got to travel a bit. In one of my travels abroad, I met a Civil Engineer of Indian origin. I shared with him the final design. He advised me to hire a good architect and engineer to construct the house, as building a sloping roof with reinforced concrete was tricky business. After returning to India, I discussed the plan again with the architect. He was based out of Vishakhapatnam. I voiced my concerns about how he would complete the project from there. He said he could easily manage without being on site. I had my apprehensions about this way of working and decided to take a second opinion. I took the designs to an architect in Kakinada and asked him to construct the house for me. He considered the plan and offered me other options for the sloping roof. He showed me his under-construction projects that flaunted a height of 18 feet in the living room. He didn't seem confident about the sloping roof. I agreed with him and assigned him the job of constructing the house exactly as per the finalized plan, sans the sloping roof.

The construction started in 1989 and so did my lessons about life in India. In the time it took to build the house, I experienced the work ethic in India, the materials used for construction and the attitude of the people. I had many grievances but sadly no choice but to put up with them.

I took a keen interest in the construction and interiors

of the house. My nephew Rajendra and I planned many things together such as the doors, windows, shutters, bathrooms, etc. We preferred not conferring with the architect quite often, as his philosophy was totally different from ours. I thought that it was my house, a place where I will be living, so it should be designed according to my tastes. Sadly, the architect thought otherwise.

When we started expressing our choices in fittings and fixtures, the architect got offended. 'You can do everything on your own; you don't need me anymore,' he said, and left in a huff. This kind of attitude is very common in India. As soon as one becomes an established professional, he starts thinking of himself as a demi-god. I cannot put up with this kind of attitude.

When the architect left the project midway, I went ahead and completed it on my own with the help of an elderly mason and his two sons. I also had an excellent carpenter called Bhaskar working for me who was able to incorporate my ideas while making the doors and furniture. The construction was almost complete by early 1991, which is when I decided to move in.

Living Conditions

Before I could move in, a storm besieged Kakinada. This must have been in May of 1990. We had just returned from a wedding in Chennai and heard of a storm brewing in the Bay of Bengal. The coast of Kakinada was subjected to heavy downpour and harsh winds for nine consecutive days.

I had never seen so much water in my life! Due to the storm, the power and water supply was cut off. Thankfully, we had stocked up on supplies. But it was difficult to store anything for long with no electricity, refrigerator or cooking stoves. Luckily, we had a bore pump in the compound, so we managed to scrape through the storm.

The storm isolated Kakinada and turned it into an island. The area where the construction was going on was completely submerged. We couldn't reach the site and there was no other means of communication. I had hired a watchman at the site who came over on his bike to update me about the status quo. According to him, there was water everywhere but our stock of cement was safe on the upper shelves of a shed. Since no construction work was actually going on at that time, the loss was minimal.

This experience taught me about how resilient our people were. A natural calamity can paralyze the lives of those affected by it, but we had the patience and tolerance to survive under harsh conditions.

I moved into my new house in early 1991. Although a lot of work remained to be done, I began living there.

It took another year for the carpenters to finish the woodwork.

Living in Canada for twenty-two years had left a deep impact on me. There were many things from my life in Canada that I wanted to bring back with me. For instance, I like simple wooden furniture. To ensure that the furniture turned out exactly as I wanted it to, I had to constantly supervise the workers. This tedious process taught me a great deal. I learnt to be more patient with people.

Even after twenty-five years, I still find that there is always something new to learn from life in India.

A New Vision

In 1991, the construction of the orphanage began. I decided to build it 20 feet away from my home. This was my dream, and I wanted to be as close to it as possible. Since I had worked with the Canadian couple who ran a children's home in Hyderabad, it was my only point of reference. I knew the drawbacks of their system and wanted to better it. However, I did not do any other research. Apart from my vision, I had no other light to guide me.

I decided to start with twenty children. The orphanage is built like a traditional Indian home, with a courtyard in the middle, and rooms on all sides.

While the orphanage was under construction, I decided to interact with the locals, and understand the conditions in which they led their lives.

This exercise proved to be an eye-opener. Most people lived in small thatched-roof houses. A family of five or six lived without toilet facilities, running water or power. There was no public transportation and hardly any pukka roads. The nearest hospital was around 15 km away, and the sick and ailing had to take a rough bicycle ride to reach the closest bus stop.

There was a Gram Panchayat school, barely 200 yards from my house, with two classrooms and two teachers. They taught 130 children and worked from 9 a.m. to 3.30 p.m.

I often came across little boys and girls driving cattle through the fields. Their clothes would be torn and they had no footwear on. With sticks in their hands and laughter in their voices, they would spend the entire day in the sun. Once I stopped by to talk to them.

Me: Why are all of you in the field and not at the school?

Little boy: My father has asked me to mind the buffaloes.

Me: Don't you want to go to school? To study?

Little girl: I want to, but my father says it's no good going to school. I am more useful in the fields than at the school. How can I go to school when I have to work in the field during the day time?

Me: You have to work in the fields during the day but you are free in the evenings, right? Would you like to come over to my house every evening and I will teach you to read and write?

All of them shouted 'Yes' in unison, their dirty faces beaming with hope and happiness. Their eagerness to learn encouraged me in my vision to change the way education is perceived in India.

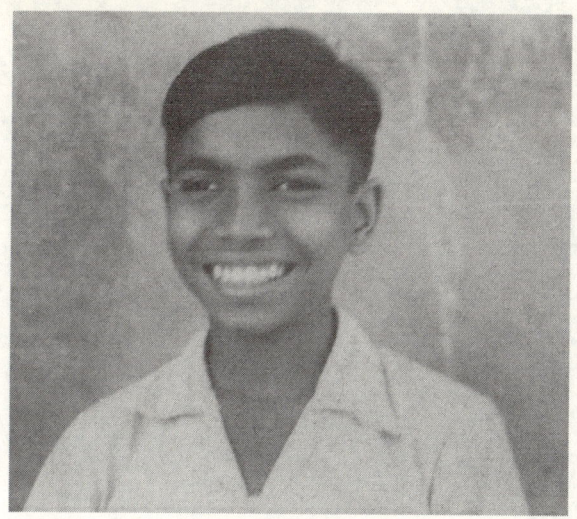

Me, at thirteen

My brother, S. Venkata Rao

My sister Padma, whom I miss even today

My sister, Hema

With batchmates of M.Sc. in Zoology at Andhra University, 1964

Manju with her brothers Durgaprasad and Bhavaniprasad when she was nine years old

Erskine College at Andhra University where I did my B.Sc. (Hons) and M.Sc. in Zoology

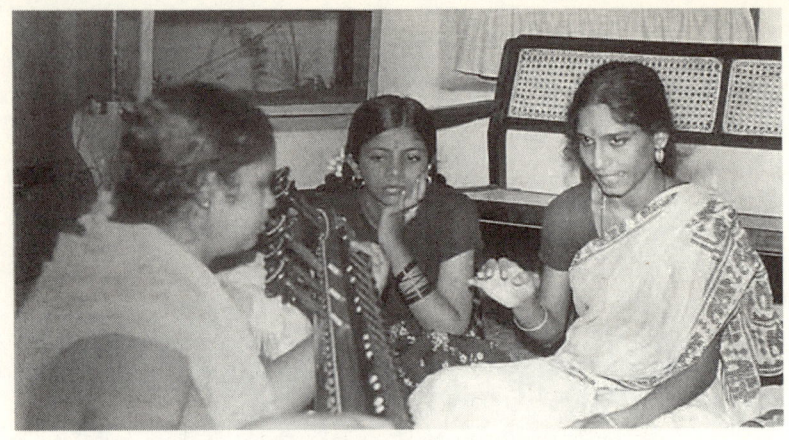

Manju learning music from her sister Mani,
while her niece Padmini watches

Our wedding at Kakinada, May 1975

My sister-in-law, S. Kausalya

At our wedding reception in Hyderabad, 14 May 1975

During our visit to India, January 1982

Our family with my in-laws at Kakinada, 1982

My kids and me on a happy occasion

Srikiran and Sarada were always posing for my camera

Sarada, Srikiran

One my best photographs of Manju, taken in Nanaimo, 1975

Srikiran (first row, second from left) in his class photograph 1983-84

My family

Air India Memorial at Cork, Ireland

At the Memorial in Cork, Ireland, on the twenty-fifth anniversary of the crash

Srikiran Eye Hospital, 1993

The new hospital building, 2005

Children at Sarada Vidyalayam school

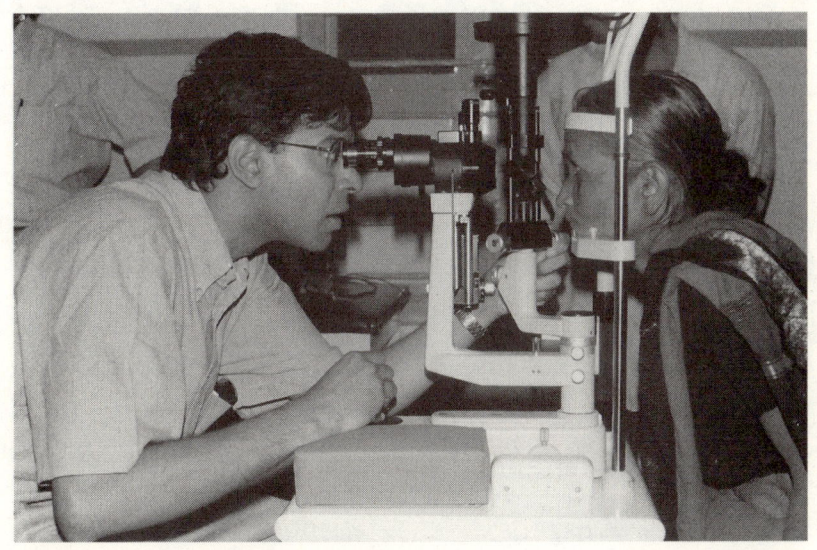

Dr. Vinod Mootha, ophthalmologist volunteer in the outpatient clinic

Dr. Kjell Dahlen, Rotarian and volunteer, along with his colleague during one of his visits to Srikiran Eye Hospital

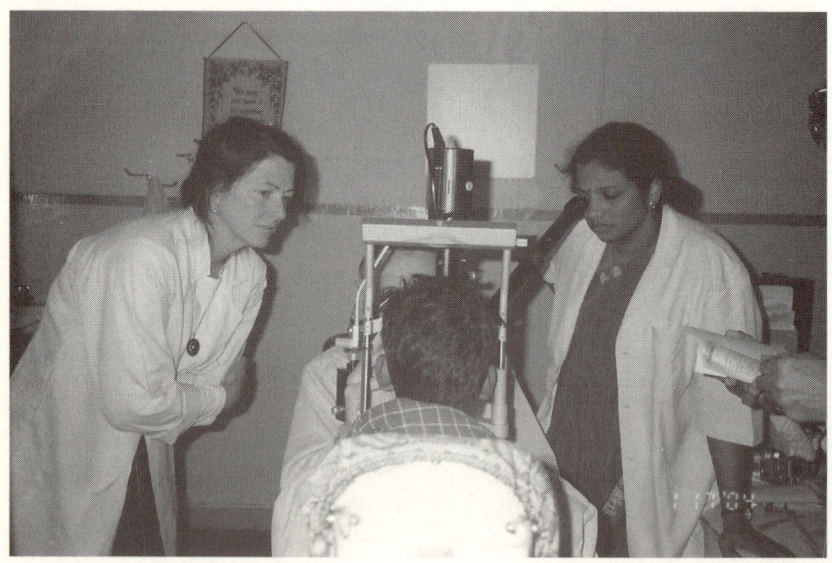

Dr. Linda Lawrence, ophthalmologist from Kansas, USA, who started the ophthalmology department at the eye hospital

Pierre Barbeau, from Help the Aged Canada, at an eye camp in India

Joseph Caron, Canadian High Commissioner to India, and his wife, Kumru Caron

Receiving an award from Satish Chandra, IAS, District Collector of East Godavari District, at a rural eye camp

Patients waiting to be examined at an eye camp

Interacting with patients at an eye camp

Non-formal education for children, 1991

Schoolchildren at a rural eye camp

Patients going home after cataract surgery

chapter five

Setting the Foundation for Sarada Vidyalayam

I once read a quote by Nelson Mandela—'Education is the most powerful weapon, which you can use to change the world.' Changing the world was far from my mind when I started teaching the farmers' children at Kakinada.

The children agreed to come at five in the evening, after finishing their work, to study at my house. My only condition was that they should have a bath before coming to study at my place.

So, at five in the evening, the porch would be filled with twenty-five eager-to-learn boys and girls, aged between five to fourteen. I began teaching them the Telugu alphabet, words, pronunciations, numbers and basic addition and subtraction. I was touched to see their motivation and enthusiasm for learning. They came every day without fail. However, on Sundays, I asked them to watch the weekly Telugu movie on Doordarshan. Since not many people had a TV in their homes in those days, watching a movie every Sunday was a big treat. It also gave me an opportunity to have time for myself.

As my unique home school evolved, I kept an eye on the students who attended the Panchayat School nearby. Often, I would interact with them and ask them to write down their names and addresses on a slate. I realized that they hadn't learnt to write properly. So, my sister Hema began offering them after-school tutorials.

From 3.30 p.m. onwards, Hema akka would be their teacher. She used to sit under the mango tree in the courtyard with forty school kids surrounding her. She, too, started with the basics of Telugu and Maths. Slowly, the children started dropping out and we were left with nineteen kids who were committed to learning.

While working at the grassroots level, I realized that these children were caught in a vicious circle. They belonged to labour class families such as carpenters and masons. Since the parents were not educated, they did not realize the importance of educating their children. This made the children drop out of school sooner or later, with most of them not even able to complete high school. And due to their lack of education, they would eventually end up in the labour market. Education was the key.

Soon we realized that an orphanage was not the

right fit for a place like Kakinada. With an orphanage, I would take responsibility for maybe twenty kids from childhood to maturity. With a school, I could help thousands of children. So, we put aside our original plan. Instead, we decided to convert the building into a primary school with Class 1 in 1992.

I remember the first day of Sarada Vidyalayam so clearly. It was Gurupurnima. The school was inaugurated by my friend and retired marine engineer Mr. Phani Babu. I had finally fulfilled my dream of setting up a school that's free for all children.

But to continue to do what I wanted, I knew I required funds. In 1989, I registered the Manjari Sankurathri Memorial Foundation (MSMF) as a Canadian charity organization to raise funds from my well-wishers in Canada. In India, I started the Sankurathri Foundation as a trust to implement the MSMF projects. Today, Sarada Vidyalayam, Srikiran Institute of Ophthalmology and Spandana, the Disaster Relief Programme, all operate under the Sankurathri Foundation.

Establishing the School

To develop the school, Hema akka and I visited many other schools. And we combined our experiences to create a teaching methodology for Sarada Vidyalayam.

In this process, we got a lot of help from

Dr. D. Shyamala, a Ph.D. in Telugu from Satya Sai Institute in Anantapur. Dr. Shyamala had many interesting ideas about education, discipline and about instilling moral values among the children.

But we had to face several challenges along the way such as finding proper teachers, grooming and retaining them. Today, I employ many of my ex-students as teachers!

No matter what the obstacle, we always carried on. Our students always fared well in public examinations, with the highest marks, between 85–95 per cent.

From Class 1, we progressed gradually to Class 7. After the students entered the Class 8, the children would have to join other high schools. But they were not happy with the quality of education imparted there. In fact, at other schools, our students would miss the personal attention they would receive from the teachers at Sarada Vidyalayam. Many parents also requested us to start a high school. So, in 2007, we began the construction of the high school building with the support from MSMF Canada.

According to me, the progress we made in those fourteen years is a commendable achievement considering the background these children hail from and the lack of support from their parents. Every child can excel given the right opportunity and that's what we demonstrate at Sarada Vidyalayam. People often think their children don't excel in school because they are not intelligent enough. But we feel that each child has a unique set of skills, which need to be honed and challenged. You need to constantly motivate them. Not all children do well in studies; some are proficient in extra-curricular activities such as drawing, painting, gardening, and sports. If we take good care of them and offer them the right opportunities, every child can stand out.

At Sarada Vidyalayam, the students learn yoga, music and Kuchipudi. Our aim is to expose the children to different vocations. If they like one of them, they can specialize in it. And we have seen this method work, time and time again. Most of the students are good at drawing, some are good orators, while others write excellent essays. Every child goes back home with awards and certificates. At the end of the day, our students get all-round development and are taught good manners and values.

Here's an example of the high values our students have. Every Diwali, we explain to them how burning crackers is harmful for the environment. Even if the elders in their family want to buy crackers, we suggest that they ask them to buy something more useful with the money. So, after Diwali, the children get the money they did not waste on crackers and put it in the Diwali collection box. On an average, we get Rs. 7,000 from this box. When we ask them what should be done with this money and their spontaneous reaction is 'Let's give this money to a blind child so that he can see again.'

We usually give three sets of uniforms to each child. At the end of the academic year, we tell the students to wash the clothes, iron them, and return them to the school. When the new academic year begins, we buy them a new set of clothes as most kids grow out of the clothes. But since the old ones are still in a good condition, we ask them what should be done with them. Without hesitation, they tell us to give them to poor children. So, we take the children along to distribute their old uniforms in government schools, orphanages, or schools for the differently abled.

Similarly, our children go to the nearby Panchayat School on a pre-decided date to host sports and quiz competitions. They also distribute sweets and chocolates to the kids. Through such activities, the students learn to contribute to the community and learn not to be self-centred.

During the Ganesh festival, we teach the kids that plaster of paris idols pollute water bodies. Instead, we encourage them to make small Ganpati idols using black clay from a nearby field. They create 150–200 idols, decorate them, and then gift them to their teachers and other staff members.

Another of our initiatives at Sarada Vidyalayam involves teaching the students to grow tulsi plants in small bags. Then they are taught the medical benefits of tulsi. Every Sunday, the students distribute these packets in their neighbourhood. They also explain the benefits of Tulsi and the importance of hygiene and sanitation. In this way, not only are the children made more conscious about healthcare and sanitation, but they are able to convey these ideas to their family and neighbours, too. Our social ideas and messages reach out to the mass rural populace of the Kakinada region through these children. What could be a better medium than this?

Remaining Focused

Sometimes I wish I could reach out to more children. Many people who visit the school ask me why I don't open branches in other areas. But I respect the self-imposed limitations of our set-up. We want to maintain high standards and ethics in whatever we do and want to work only with people with integrity.

Since its inception, we have evolved several methods and initiatives for the school's system. One of the major initiatives was the decision to involve parents in the working of the school. We did this by organizing parent committees in each of the six villages that housed the students. Each village is represented by one parent who is selected by the others to be in-charge. The parents meet on the first Sunday of each month to discuss various issues involving the school, students and parents. The following Monday, the spokesperson visits the school at 2.30 p.m. and meets the management personnel. If any parent fails to attend the meeting on Sunday, they have to come to school on Monday afternoon to inform us why they couldn't attend the meeting. As most of the parents want to avoid coming to the school and offer explanations for their absence, they attend the meeting on Sunday. In this manner, we instil discipline among the parents. In this meeting, they exchange ideas, address complaints and sort out parent–teacher issues. These committee meetings have proved to be very useful in building a cohesive network amongst parents.

Most of the parents are very co-operative because they believe their children are getting a good education at Sarada Vidyalayam. We have also noticed the growing interest of parents in their children's well-being. We encourage the students to go home and brief the parents every day on what they did at school, while at the same time urging the parents to proactively participate in their children's studies. This is an important factor in the development of the child, because most of these children feel their parents don't attend to their needs or take proper care of them. Apart from the committee meetings, we also have general meetings where all the parents are invited to come and meet the teachers and school's management. In the general meeting, we discuss about how the children are behaving, how the outside world is changing, and how they should protect their children.

We also tell the parents to be alert and to monitor what their children are doing in their free time so that they are safe from bad influences. At school, all of them are well-protected, and we don't want them to get hurt in the outside world.

In the general meetings, many parents express joy that their children are learning many good things such as keeping the house clean, saving water, and planting trees. Not only that, they also realize that Sarada Vidyalayam's students are different from others.

An important milestone for us was when we achieved a zero-dropout rate, especially since almost 60–70 per cent of our students are girls. One of the reasons for this is the confidence parents have in the safety standards of our school. Girls in rural areas are generally married off at a young age. But Sarada Vidyalayam girls have continued studies beyond Class 10, even at the intermediate level, and in professional courses. By the time they finish their education, they are above twenty-one years of age and well above the legal marriageable age. Educating a girl child in rural areas helps fight the dual evils of child labour and child marriage. An educated girl has the capability to be financially independent and socially responsible; she becomes the building block of a better home and a better community.

My little girl Sarada always wanted to go to school. But she couldn't. There was no second thought about what the name of the school should be. I feel that Sarada would have been so happy to see the children of Kakinada go to such a worthy school, that's named after her.

chapter six

Braving All Odds

Children have the capacity to bring immense joy to their parents. A toddler's smile, a teenager's sports trophy or the first pay cheque of a fresh graduate can make any parent proud. I may not have Srikiran and Sarada with me but I am not bereft of parental joy and pride. Today, when I look at the students of Sarada Vidyalayam, I feel deep satisfaction. After finishing schooling, they secure admission in government polytechnic institutes and continue with higher studies. By providing quality education, we have managed to make education accessible and affordable to all. Schooling at Sarada Vidyalayam amounts to Rs. 10,000–15,000 per year and the Sankurathri Foundation also gives the students scholarships for higher education.

Our ex-students visit us regularly. We are filled with joy at every success story. It makes us proud to see the children all grown up, ably shouldering responsibilities of marriage, job and families.

One student, Padala Murli Krishna, completed his mechanical engineering diploma at Andhra Polytechnic Institute, appeared for his ECET exams (Engineering Common Entrance Test) and got admission in B. Tech at Bhimavaram. He stood second in the state in the polytechnic final year, and in the B. Tech exams he won the gold medal. He was the first student to get a grade point average of 10 from the college!

As job offers started pouring in, he came to consult me. I advised him to opt for Larsen & Toubro. In the meantime, he received an offer from a very prestigious organization called Indian Space Research Organization (ISRO), which is the equivalent of NASA in the USA. This was an incredible opportunity. He is currently working as an engineer there. He is a role model for all the students at Sarada Vidyalayam.

Another brilliant student was Golapalli Rama Ganga. A software engineer, he is currently working with a multi-national company in Kuala Lumpur, Malaysia. Whenever he comes to meet his parents in the village, he visits the Foundation.

We once had a student called Jakkilenki Renuka Ganga. She studied in our school till Class 7 and was an excellent student. Since we did not have a high school back then, we encouraged her to join a private school. Her education at Sarada Vidyalayam had been in Telugu but the new school was an English medium one. Within three months of joining the new school, she topped her class. She remained at the top of her class all through high school. She scored full marks in Mathematics in SSC exams. Subsequently, she secured admission at a government college in Kakinada.

After completing her B. Tech. degree, she was offered a job by Capgemini, a multi-national software company, in Mumbai. She, too, makes it a point to visit the Foundation and meet us every time she is in Kakinada.

Another inspiring story is that of a boy named Kumar who joined our school in Class 1. His father had abandoned him and his mother. She was forced to work as a janitor at the Foundation. He was a mischievous but intelligent child. He completed Class 7 with good marks and went to A.P. Residential School Bhupathipalem for further studies. Later, he got into a polytechnic college in Kakinada. While in his final year, he was offered a job during campus placements at ITC in Bhadrachalam. I still remember the conversation I had with him.

Me: Congratulations Kumar!

Kumar: Thank you, Sir.

Me: You bagged an excellent offer. What are your plans now?

Kumar: I will work hard to the best of my capacity, Sir. I will make sure I earn a name for myself with hard work and honesty.

Me: And what about your mother?

Kumar: The days of her struggle are over. From now on, she will not need to work for a single day. I will take her with me wherever I go.

Hearing his answer, I was filled with immense satisfaction. The efforts we had put in our students at Sarada Vidyalayam were bearing fruit.

Often, when I look at students from other schools or young professionals, I find that they lack good values. That's why we made it a point to focus on the overall development of students rather than just academic progress. Not all of our students have been able to pursue further studies or take up professional courses. Some started doing a business, while others got into teaching. But all of them are doing well in their lives. We tell our kids that it is not necessary for everyone to be doctors or engineers, but whatever they decide to do in life should be done with diligence.

However, there is one problem that I still wish to solve. When our children leave for high school, they struggle with learning in English. Many of them feel shy and hesitant due to this. So, I am planning to start an English medium high school.

This will take some time, but one day I know my dream will come true.

Expanding the Horizon

Initially, we taught only till Class 7. However, many parents came to us saying that their children were not happy at other schools.

'Please start a high school,' they pleaded. But, due to lack of funds and unavailability of good teachers, we could not expand the school.

A year later, in 2007, I met an interesting person—Noordin Matadali—who changed everything at school. I was in Vancouver, making a presentation on the Foundation. Noordin walked up to me and introduced himself.

'Dr. Chandra, I would like to come and volunteer at your Foundation,' he said. Noordin was an accountant—I was sceptical about what he could contribute. But, he kept his word and came down with his wife, Guli, to the Foundation on 7 November 2008. They stayed with us for three days, and observed all activities—the eye camps, the hospital and the school. On his last day, we sat together on the porch to discuss his visit.

Noordin: Chandra, I am impressed with the Foundation's work.

Me: I am sure you got to see much more than what was shown in the CBC documentary—A Ray of Light.

Noordin: Oh certainly! Chandra, is there anything I can do for you to help you?

Me: Sure, you can. I am here in India, but the Manjari Sankurathri Memorial Foundation is in Canada. We are trying to raise funds there, but we don't have anyone to manage the activities. Help us in promoting the activities of the Foundation among your friends and relatives in Vancouver.

True to his word, Noordin worked hard to raise funds in Canada. He even sent a $50,000 cheque to our Foundation in Ottawa.

One day he called me, 'Chandra, I want to do much more for your Foundation because you can do better work in the field of education and healthcare.'

I took his words as good wishes, without knowing their true import.

On Noordin's sixty-fifth birthday, he had invited me as the guest of honour. The celebrations were planned at several locations—each day at a different place where he invited his friends and acquaintances. At each event, he would talk about the Sankurathri Foundation with his guests. I, too, would briefly speak about our work.

A week later, the donations started pouring in. We raised $250,000. Finally, I had the means to start the high school!

Without Noordin, my dream of a high school would have remained unfulfilled. The high school was inaugurated by Dr. Allam Apparao, Vice Chancellor,

JNTUK (Jawaharlal Nehru Technological University Kakinada) on 27 November 2009.

Today, as students successfully pass out of the Sarada Vidyalayam high school, I miss having Noordin around to share the happiness. Sadly, he passed away in 2014.

Overcoming Obstacles

Teachers are the soul of any school. Training them to guide the children properly, to help them realize their true potential, became our fundamental concern.

Initially, we decided to hire inexperienced people, so we could mould them the way we saw fit. As long as they could be good mentors for the children, their qualifications made no difference to us.

Since our first year itself, we saw how much the children enjoyed coming to school. Their home life was far from ideal. Their parents worked as labourers and didn't have time to look after them properly. But at school, they felt taken care of.

We also made it very clear to our teachers that no corporal punishments would be permitted. The teachers always talk affectionately to the students. Maybe that's why we have 100 per cent attendance in the school.

What's more, we have never ever had a single case of any student dropping out of school! When the national average is a dismal 65 per cent, our 0 per cent dropout rate is astounding.

Perhaps our advocacy work with the Akshaya Patra Foundation, an NGO that runs the largest midday meal programme, has also helped. The midday meal is not only an incentive for the students to attend school every day, but it also takes care of their nutrition.

In the past five–six years, I have noticed a big change in the people around here. TV and Internet have opened up new vistas for these people. Owning a TV is seen as a sign of progress. But, on the flipside, I see many parents neglecting their children because they are far too engrossed in watching the mindless entertainment on TV.

As the future unfolds, we will see how we can maintain our standards, how we can instil in our students the values we believe in, and how we can mould them to be good citizens of the world.

chapter seven

Forming a Vision

Kakinada is a beautiful place, but life in the village can be truly wretched. There was a lack of basic healthcare facilities—the poor villagers would have to cycle many kilometres to reach the nearest bus stop, and then take the bus to the hospital. It would cost them a day's wages.

My childhood friend, Dr. V.K. Raju, a practicing ophthalmologist in the US, used to visit Andhra Pradesh, especially Vijaywada, to organize eye camps. He would spend two–three weeks in India helping the rural populace, mostly children, who couldn't afford eye treatments. However, he found the whole exercise quite frustrating. He would treat the patients during the eye camp, but there was no way for them to do follow-up treatment. As a result, the conditions tended to relapse.

I thought a great deal about this problem and decided

... why not start an eye hospital! Since I was based in Kakinada, I could look after the hospital in Raju's absence. Initially, he was hesitant, but I was able to convince him.

The year was 1992. Right from day one, we were clear about what we wanted—to provide quality eye care that is accessible and affordable for rural people. We paid a lot of attention to quality. Whether the patient paid money or not, he would always receive high quality of care.

Starting the Groundwork

The first step was to find a well-trained ophthalmologist to head the medical procedures in Raju's absence. I would look after the hospital management. I found a young, capable doctor and sent him to train under Dr. Raju in the US. At that time, we had no external funding for the hospital and all his expenses were paid for by us. He stayed with Raju for almost a year. By the time he returned, in 1993, our school building was ready. Since we did not have any other facility, we decided to have the eye hospital on the first floor and the school on the ground floor.

As with Sarada Vidyalayam, there was no doubt in my mind about the name the hospital. It was christened Srikiran Institute of Ophthalmology. Mr. Randeep

Sudan, IAS, district collector, inaugurated the hospital on 21 January 1993.

Right from its inception, the hospital was supported by the Eye Foundation of America. We began conducting community outreach programmes in the nearby village. At the first eye camp, we scanned fifty-six patients and identified nine cataract cases. We brought them to the hospital in my Maruti Gypsy, a four-wheel drive vehicle, and performed the first intraocular lens (IOL) implant in Kakinada.

From the very beginning, the hospital picked up momentum. The outpatient clinic was open from 8.30 a.m. to 5.30 p.m. Despite poor transportation and roads, patients would walk in, come rain or shine. Seeing the sheer number of patients in various stages of blindness come to us for help, shook me. And I was glad that we had built a hospital that could bring light to so many lives.

With such high demand for the hospital, it was getting difficult to co-share the building with the school. Soon we started work on the new school building in the south-east corner of the estate and, eventually, the children were moved into the new building. The hospital was then spread across two floors, with the OPD, vision testing, reception, pharmacy and optical shop on the ground floor, and one operation theatre with adjoining scrub room and sterilization room as well as three private rooms, single rooms and one large shared accommodation room on the first floor. This is how the hospital functioned till 1994.

But as the hospital's popularity increased, our problems escalated.

Taking Hurdles Head-On

The Foundation had only one vehicle at its disposal—my personal Maruti Gypsy—which was used to pick and drop patients. But it was proving to be difficult to manage the workload. We sometimes hired private transportation, which was risky and expensive. Finally, we received Rs. 250,000 as a donation from Jindal Aluminium to buy a bus. But we were falling short by Rs. 250,000 since the bus cost was more than Rs. 5 lakhs. Hence, I decided to sell the Gypsy and contribute towards the proceeds.

In the beginning, we had a small team of employees. But since the entire hospital was run using my personal finance, it was getting increasingly difficult to make ends meet. Paying the staff salaries at the end of the month was always a daunting task. However, it was a rule that I was clear about when the hospital started, that every staff member would get his or her salary on the last day of the month. That's a rule we adhere to till today. Some people thought that I had made a large amount of money in Canada, while others were of the opinion that I received largesse from my Canadian friends. But no one knew the inside story.

To manage the hospital, I appointed a man named Madhu as the administrator for the hospital. He was sent to the Aravind Eye Care hospital in Madurai to do the administrator's course. I, too, got an opportunity to meet Dr. G. Venkataswamy of Aravind Eye Care and remember his encouraging words very well.

Donations of Every Kind

In spite of the financial restrictions, we were running both the school and hospital fairly smoothly. We did not ask for donations nor did we publicize our work. We were definitely not making any profit, but the satisfaction we drew from our work was immense.

Over the years, there have been many instances when the poor and needy have shown us a very different side of humanity. Once an elderly woman, who lived with her widowed daughter and did household work for Rs. 30 per month, insisted on making a donation to us. I gently refused her saying we don't accept donations from the patients. But she persisted. All she wanted to do was donate a month's salary to the hospital that helped her regain her eyesight.

On the other hand, there have been some unsavoury

incidents as well. Once a god-man visited the hospital along with his followers. After the check-up, we realized that he had cataract. After a successful operation, he tried offering money to the ward nurses, who refused to take it. Their refusal made him furious. How can anyone refuse his money, his 'prasadam', he yelled!

But we remained steadfast. No employee at Srikiran Hospital accepts money from patients, not even as a tip, because that breeds corruption. I know how rampant corruption is in India, and I want to prove to the world that things can improve.

Despite our good work, many people remained sceptical about our intentions. 'This man isn't from here, so why does he want to do so much for us?' they whispered. To clear their doubts, I decided to hang a picture of Manju, Srikiran and Sarada in the hospital. A note in English and Telugu explained that the hospital had been founded in the memory of my family who died in the Air India plane crash. Some were convinced by this, but others remained suspicious. They thought I had a lot of money stashed away somewhere which I was using to finance the hospital.

Nothing could have been further from the truth.

The budget of Rs. 20 lakh per year had doubled since the number of patients had grown. Luckily, in 1997, I came across an NGO called Help the Aged Canada, based in Ottawa. We sent them a proposal about our work in providing free cataract surgeries to elderly people. The NGO liked our proposal and decided to give us a grant—of CAD 200,000. It was a big boost for our young organization!

We also got three more projects from the Canadian International Development Agency (CIDA). With that money we could build infrastructure, procure equipment, and strengthen our fragile financial system. The grants helped us train more ophthalmic assistants and increase our community outreach programme.

Encouraged by this, I became more active in the field of fundraising. Every year I would go to Canada and make presentations. MSMF was registered as a charitable organization, and the money donated to MSMF was used for the various activities of the Sankurathri Foundation in India.

Apart from the monetary support that we received from our collaborators abroad, we also hosted volunteers who came to work with us as eye care professionals. Dr. Kjell Dhalen, a prominent ophthalmologist from Eye Care for Adirondacks, New York, visited us as a volunteer and continued coming back to the hospital for the next eighteen years!

In 1994 and 1995, the hospital grew considerably, and we bought many new machines such as the Argon Laser machine to treat diabetic retinopathy. Phaco surgery for cataract was conducted by Raju for the first time in the Kakinada region. We also added textbooks, ophthalmic journals and video cassettes to our library. The Srikiran Institute of Ophthalmology also received a boost when we started our first fellowship programme in Comprehensive Ophthalmology.

Learning Process

There is always something new to learn at the Srikiran Institute of Ophthalmology. Through the Foundation, I met many people including doctors, IT personnel, international volunteers, ophthalmologists, teachers and philanthropists. But what I enjoyed the most was meeting young people, filled with dreams and new ideas. It has been my mission to empower the rural youth—with education, employment, values and ambition.

Today, when I look back at all the struggles we faced in the initial phase of the hospital, I am amazed at how we managed to pull through. The efforts of the hospital staff, my well-wishers in India and Canada, and the villagers have paid fruitful dividends. I am happy with the progress we have made, but given my nature, I think we can still do more. Much more.

chapter eight

Fulfilling the Vision

On one of my trips to a nearby village, I came across a young man begging on the road. He was broadly built and looked healthy and strong. I was wondering why such a strapping young boy was begging on the streets. I asked one of my staff members to investigate and we discovered that he was blinded by cataract. We immediately took him with us to the hospital and within a day, his cataract removal surgery was performed. He was ecstatic on recovering his eyesight. With tears of gratitude in his eyes, he said that he would get back to working and earning a living. Such a response from our patients gives me immense satisfaction. I am proud of the fact that we are not only helping people regain their vision but also putting them back into the economy.

For us, the people who come to the hospital are not just patients, they are human stories. The plight of the poor of India who are plunged into meaningless blindness tells the tale of our shortcomings as a nation. Having lived in Canada where quality healthcare is provided to every individual, be it a citizen or a migrant, it pains me to see so many Indians bereft of basic medical facilities. Already living in the throes of poverty, people in the villages affected by cataract lose not just their vision but also their hope for survival. They become dependent on their kin, are physically incapable of providing for themselves, and are often seen as a burden on their families. And by that I don't mean just older folks; even the young are victims of cataract. They continue to live in this abject state without realizing that there is a way out. Recently, we had a patient who had gone blind in both his eyes because of cataract. His wife took their child with her when she left him. He somehow found his way to the hospital where he was treated. Upon regaining his eyesight, he said he would go looking for his wife and child.

Expanding Our Reach

Now let me go back to the story of the hospital's development over the years. Within three years of the hospital being operational, the patient load doubled and the current capacity quickly became inadequate. In 1996, we added the second floor to the hospital building. A new building was built to accommodate the canteen, optical, pharmacy and nurses' quarters.

I tried to keep the hospital as up-to-date as possible and introduced new instruments, within the limited scope of our resources. For instance, in 1997 we installed the Carl-Zeiss Microscope with camera and other accessories. This was through the International Rotary grant from Dr. Dahlen, Plattsburgh, New York. Later in the year, a team from Christoffel Blinden Mission (CBM), Germany, visited us to explore the possibilities of partnerships.

For us, 1997 was a landmark year. We started Small Incision Cataract Surgery (SICS) for the first time in the region and it became a standard in eye care for us. The number of surgeries crossed five hundred per month for the first time in 1997. Srikiran Hospital successfully implanted intraocular lenses for 95 per cent of the patients, whereas the national average was 55 per cent.

In 1998, Raju operated on Sri K. V. R. Chowdary, chairman, SMRT. It was a Phaco Surgery done under topical anaesthesia. He was impressed with the facility and decided to donate two used buses for the transportation of patients from the villages for free treatment. That boosted our patient outreach programme as we were able to engage with more villages and bring more patients over to the hospital for treatment. Later that year, we also installed the Zeiss Yag Laser machine. By 1998, we had crossed over 1,000 surgeries per month.

At Srikiran Hospital, it is our constant endeavour to

upgrade our systems, procedures and services. We keep the hospital abreast with the latest innovation in eye care and incorporate new technology and machinery to the best of our ability. For instance, we started the telemedicine programme at the hospital, which was launched by Dr. Linda Lawrence from Salina, Kansas, USA, and the glaucoma programme by Dr. R. Ramakrishnan, Aravind Eye Hospital, Tirunelveli, Tamil Nadu.

As the hospital grew, I realized the importance of having end-to-end solutions for everything that we needed for our activities within our premises. That's why today we have the nurses' quarters, the optical shop, the automated spectacle surfacing unit, the kitchen and canteen and also a separate structure for generators, washing machines and dryers, all located in, or near, the hospital buildings.

Although we had two temporary high-tech shacks to accommodate more in-patients, the facility was falling short for the rising influx of patients. We were considering the possibility of an extension to the old building. Once sufficient funds were in place, thanks to MSMF, we started the construction work. This was in 2001. In the same year, the surgeries per year reached a staggering number of 16,726! Srikiran Hospital received the Best NGO Award for performing the maximum number of cataract surgeries for two consecutive years.

It was also recognized as a training centre for sponsored eye doctors by the Ministry of Health, India.

The new hospital building was ready in 2004. It is spread across 40,000 square feet. Apart from four operation theatres, the new building has large waiting areas that provide ample space for outpatients and comfortable rooms for inpatients. There are plenty of single and double rooms for the paid patients. With every aspect of the hospital's functions getting a dedicated space, it was possible for us to add specialty clinics such as the dry eye clinic. Since the majority of the patients coming to us are illiterate, it is important for us to keep their medical records with us, which are preserved in both hard and soft formats for reference.

With the facility expanding, we naturally increased the number of staff to handle the increasing workload. While most of the staff members are experienced hands, we conduct induction programmes for them once they join us. The way Srikiran Hospital works is unique and each person working here needs to be entrenched in its methodology.

Long-term Planning

A young woman once came to the hospital carrying a one-year-old boy. The little one was blind in both the eyes due to corneal opacities. Since his corneas were white, his parents had probably found it hard to come to terms with it. The woman who brought her to us had found this abandoned baby and adopted him. Although not well-off herself, she took it upon herself to raise the baby and get his eyes treated. She came to us after many disappointing visits to government and private hospitals where she was quoted enormous amounts for required corneal transplant. When she came to us, our cornea specialist confirmed that the boy's eyesight could be restored with corneal transplants. We went ahead with his surgeries, which were done completely free. Both the corneas were transplanted successfully in two separate operations. Today, the boy is able to see. He comes for regular check-ups and leads a happy life with his adopted mother.

This boy's story is a perfect example of medical expertise and human compassion. I feel the woman's love for the abandoned baby would have overcome any barriers coming their way. It was her dream to see the boy get his vision back. The medical expertise of Srikiran Hospital proved instrumental in fulfilling her dream. This is just one example—there are scores of such stories that unfold at our hospital every day.

Another reason why I narrated the story here is to elaborate upon the children's eye care programme that we implemented in 2005. For this, we partnered with ORBIS. While we always had a dedicated section for kids, post 2005, we expanded this facility. We trained a special team to take this programme forward at the hospital as well as to increase the children's outreach programme in the villages.

Over the next couple of years, we reached the mark of one lakh surgeries per year and were successful in providing basic eye care to over four lakh rural people.

Although our outreach programme was doing very well, with a good turnout of people who were getting their eyes checked and treated, we realized that we needed something permanent in the long run. That's how the idea of Vision Centres came up. A Vision Centre is a touch point for people living in small towns and villages around Kakinada. The idea is to make eye care accessible to everyone all the time. Instead of waiting for an outreach camp, all they have to do is walk into the nearest Vision Centre and get a trained person to examine their eyes. We established the first four Vision Centres in 2006 in the East Godavari district. Three more centres were added in 2014. The Vision Centres were possible due to the funds raised by MSMF and CIDA. These centres provide 'closer to home' eye care six days a week.

The following year, new feathers were added to our cap with the establishment of the Retina Clinic (with the cooperation of Pushpagiri Vitreo Retina Institute, Hyderabad), SICS training for international residents in Ophthalmology from Canada and the US, and the City Centre to provide eye care to employees. In 2009, we started the Cornea Unit, Glaucoma Unit and Occuloplasty Unit. We also obtained accreditation with the National Board of Examination to start a DNB (Diplomate of National Board) degree in Ophthalmology.

The success of Srikiran Hospital and our various programmes has been the dedication of the team members, the support of our well-wishers and the processes that we have refined and established at the hospital over the years. Since the systems are in place, everyone knows what he or she has to do. This enables them to work like a unit and avoid conflicts. Right from the time the bus leaves for the eye camp till the time the patient is discharged, a fully thought-out process is strictly followed. At the eye camp, various units are set up with experts stationed at each unit to fulfil the designated task. Once the camp is underway, the patient has to first get his medical card filled, which has details about his preliminary eye check-up. Next, he is administered eye drops before the detailed examination is done. The expert checks the eyes and determines the urgency of surgery for the patient. Follow-up details are filled in the patient's card. Then a list of the patients ready for operations is compiled and the patients are ushered into the bus. No relatives are allowed to accompany the patients due to the limited space available. The patients are given food and then transferred to the hospital.

At the hospital, the patients are shown into the in-patient rooms. They spend the night there and in the morning, are readied for the surgery. The operation theatre works with industrial precision as the doctors have to finish surgeries in large numbers each day. Once the operation is done, the patients wait in the recovery room. Their dressing is removed the next morning. A preliminary examination is done and they are discharged. Throughout their stay, they are provided with food from the hospital kitchen and are given clean, hygienic rooms to live in. The last service that we provide for them is to take them back to the village in our bus.

We completed 2,00,000 surgeries on 3 August 2014 at Srikiran Hospital—an historic day for us. Over the years, our list of collaborators has grown and we have organizations such as Rotary International, Help the Aged Canada, Christoffel Blinden Mission, ORBIS, Kruti-Dhata and TOMS joining our efforts, while MSMF (Manjari Sankurathri Memorial Foundation) and CIDA (Canadian International Development Agency) continue with their endeavours. The target of 2,00,000 surgeries would not have been possible without the dedication of our team of doctors, paramedical personnel, volunteers and support staff.

Building Hands

My journey with Srikiran Institute of Ophthalmology has been a fulfilling one and continues to be so. The hospital has achieved many milestones and has been awarded and rewarded for its efforts. But that doesn't mean that the journey was without its set of challenges and hurdles. Running the hospital has always been an uphill task. Our people have been our strength. But sometimes, we've had issues too. One unfortunate event involved Raju.

The eye specialists heading the hospital were a husband–wife duo. While they were good doctors, they had certain problems with the way we worked. There came a time when our way of thinking was not in tandem anymore. Instead of sorting out the differences with me, they sought out Raju, who seemed to agree with them. Raju discussed the differences with me and although I was displeased with the way protocol had been cast aside, I tried my best to reason with him. However, he had already made up his mind by then. Raju, along with the two doctors, decided to quit the hospital. They also took with them Madhu, our administrator. They opened another charity hospital in Rajahmundry.

This was a difficult time for me, not only because we lost our senior team members but because Raju was a great friend.

But I wasn't about to let their departure compromise

the smooth running of the hospital. We quickly roped in other doctors, and stuck to the core ethics and vision that have sustained us these many years. Thus, we survived.

My experience with employees has been more good than bad. Yes, some have left us in the lurch, but many have become shining examples of dedication. For instance, Murthy is like family to us. He has been with us for more than fourteen years. Although he shifted to Vizag for a year, he came back and re-joined the hospital. He has held several designations here including that of an IT personnel and data manager. He is currently the head of the patient-counselling department. His wife is also working with us in the IT section.

One interesting case is that of Gangadhar. Young Gangadhar was five when he joined Sarada Vidyalayam. His father used to beat him up and not let him come to school. He was on the verge of giving up on his education when I met his father and drilled some sense into him. I offered him a job at the Foundation as gardener and his wife was given work in the kitchen. Gangadhar continued to study at our school till Class 7. He then finished his SSC from the Panchayat School. As soon as he passed his exams, he came to me asking for a job. Since then he has been with us, learning all aspects of the hospital's work. He has beautiful handwriting and writes proverbs on the notice board every day. When we started the automated lens system, we sent him to

Chennai to be trained. There, he learnt cost-effective methods of dispensing lens. He was managing the lens workshop and the optical shop till three years ago when we outsourced it.

Gangadhar was then put in the operation theatre as an assistant. He was sent to Aravind Eye Hospital to learn equipment maintenance. He is now with our biomedical department. Gangadhar is always the first to volunteer for our eye camps, even if they are on Sundays. He is also part of our disaster relief programme—Spandana. Such is his dedication towards me and towards the hospital!

Stronghold of Processes

Today, Srikiran Institute of Ophthalmology has eight Vision Centres catering to over ten lakh rural people. We have the only dry eye treatment centre in Andhra Pradesh. Our specialities include cornea, retina, glaucoma, occuloplasty, squint, low vision, training and research. We also have a dedicated section for paediatric eye care, which was established with the support of ORBIS, UK.

The hospital is dependent on systems that operate with clockwork precision as much as it is on the people working for it. We don't follow high-tech processes for hospital management but our system is time-tested, something which is unique to Srikiran Hospital. Every

Saturday, we have a general body meeting where every department head gets to voice his or her concerns. This allows each department to know what is happening in the rest of the hospital and what problems other staff members are facing. We evaluate monthly progress reports, too. There are currently 150 employees at Srikiran Hospital. Any one of them, from a doctor to a janitor, can approach me directly with their concerns. I wear the staff uniform and carry an identity card just like everyone else. My office, too, is in the new hospital. I think that because I am approachable to everyone, there is synergy in the hospital.

There's another great initiative that I think makes a big difference—each employee maintains a personal performance log book, which is monitored by his supervisor. This log book, along with a self-appraisal form, helps the person in-charge to evaluate the performance of the employees in his department. Based on the evaluation, increments are granted in April every year.

Provision has also been made for motivational talks, videos, presentations and open forums for the employees to voice their concerns and raise questions.

The vision with which Srikiran Hospital was built has today become a reality. But, for me, resting on our laurels is not enough. Each day is a struggle to do better, to achieve more, and to serve the people in more and more ways. Many people ask me why I don't open hospitals like Srikiran Institute of Ophthalmology in other parts of the state. I tell them that it's best that I focus on one hospital and do a good job as per the benchmarks that I have set for myself. But it will please me immensely if our hospital's work model and standards are replicated across all rural clusters of India.

I believe almost 80 per cent of blindness in India can be prevented or cured. All it takes is a dedicated effort to reach out to the masses and give them quality and affordable eye care.

chapter nine

The Way Forward

I have been born and brought up in India and it's been thirty years that I have re-settled here. But it is still difficult for me to call this place my home. I love my country and I am patriotic, too, but the ground realities of our nation leave much to be desired.

Having spent my developing years in Canada, I am able to see the vast differences between the two countries. I don't wish to bring in any comparisons here as the history and culture of India and Canada are different. But the attitude and behaviour of the people in both the countries exemplifies the level of development in them.

People in India, especially educated people, tend to be pretentious and have low integrity. They might say something and mean something completely different. There is also a tendency to please someone holding higher authority by compromising on your integrity. Running a charity foundation in India has given me the chance to observe people here at close quarters. People have absolutely no qualms about lying, cheating, blaming others for their mistakes and taking credit for something they have not done. When I initially came to Kakinada, I was so put off by the people's attitudes that I wanted to pack my bags and return to Canada. But then I realized that there are people here who truly need and deserve help. As the years passed by and the Foundation's work grew, I understood the importance of our establishment in the life of the people working here, their families and the poor rural people who benefitted from our work. To leave all this on account of some people's attitude felt wrong.

That's why I focus on building a strong moral code in the students of Sarada Vidyalayam. Once these values are inculcated from a young age, the children are likely to grow up to be responsible and proactive citizens of India.

Problem of Blindness

When I think about the reasons behind starting Srikiran Institute of Ophthalmology, I am once again astounded by the gravity of the problem of blindness in our country. Disparity of class is a universal phenomenon but it is a humongous one in India. The gulf between the rich and the poor is abysmal, leading the poor bereft of even the most basic facilities. Today, for more than two decades we have been serving the economically backward people from the rural districts around Kakinada, and still the problem of blindness persists. In spite of scaling up our facilities and reaching out to more and more rural pockets, the level of awareness about avoidable blindness continues to be negligent. According to one estimate, India has 19 million blind people, with over 80 per cent suffering from curable blindness.

The major cause of blindness in India is cataract. In our outreach programmes, we find that almost 60 per cent of the patients are suffering from cataract. It is imperative to operate on the existing cataract cases and free the patients from avoidable blindness and dependency.

When we started Srikiran Hospital, the average cost of a cataract surgery was Rs. 500. Today, thanks to inflation, it is Rs. 2,500. However, it is worth investing this much money in getting rid of cataract rather than remaining blind for the rest of your life. Unfortunately, the rural poor live in such pathetic conditions that they often can't put together Rs. 2,500 for a cataract surgery. At Srikiran Hospital, we are serving a population of close to ten million, in the east and west Godavari districts, Khamman district and Vishakhapatnam district. Besides these four districts, we get patients from all over India, too. Our main concern is to help cataract patients, restore their vision and return them into their community as productive citizens.

Several years ago, intraocular lens implant was expensive as the lens was not manufactured in India. But today it is easily available at affordable prices. So, I don't see any reason why every cataract patient shouldn't get this treatment. With such high-quality surgery and implants, the outcome will definitely be good.

The second big problem in India is glaucoma. Timely detection of glaucoma is important otherwise the patient might lose his eyesight forever. And regular eye check-ups are the only way to detect and monitor glaucoma.

Thirdly, the rise of diabetes in India means that diabetic retinopathy is an increasing form of blindness. The retina is the screen where the image is first formed. And any damage to the retina leads to loss of communication between the eye and the brain. Rectifying diabetic retinopathy requires highly trained and competent surgeons. Srikiran Hospital is one of the tertiary eye care centres in India that provides a service for people suffering from diabetic retinopathy and helps in restoring their eyesight.

Paediatric blindness and squint are problems that afflict children. Infants born with congenital cataracts need immediate surgical intervention in order to avoid complications and irreparable damage. Squint is often ignored as people regard it as a sign of luck. This could have been the case in olden times when no remedy was available. It might have boosted the confidence of the squint-eyed person. However, today it can be rectified. Apart from genetic blindness, all other eye conditions can be treated if diagnosed on time. Almost 80 per cent of the blindness we see around us can be avoided with proper surgical intervention. People need to be more aware of the solutions available. There should be facilities provided for regular eye check-ups and medical aid. With combined efforts of the people, NGOs and the government, we can eradicate this rampant problem from our country. The government has put up a concentrated effort for complete eradication of polio—a similar effort is required for cataract-led blindness.

Since the time we started Srikiran Hospital, I have faced the issue of finding qualified and competent surgeons and paramedical personnel. While the role of a surgeon is pivotal, the paramedics, too, are important. A skilled paramedic assisting the surgeon in the operation theatre is a blessing, especially in our kind of setup where cataract surgeries are done on an industrial scale and with an assembly line system. That's why we give advanced training to doctors and paramedics at the institute. We offer fellowships to recent postgraduates to improve their diagnostic and surgical skills. They usually stay with us for a year to eighteen months. During this time, they are exposed to thousands of patients in the outpatient clinic. They get ample opportunities to improve their skills in the operation theatre by working under the most experienced and competent surgeons at Srikiran Hospital. For the paramedics, we have an ophthalmic assistance course for two years. This course is focused on the impoverished youth in the state who are unable to pursue higher studies. We give them a stipend for their training-cum-internship at the institute. Students who complete this course are either absorbed in our hospital or easily get jobs in private clinics as eye technicians. Our training enables them to be the best in their field.

Spirit of Volunteering

I am often asked about what message I would like to give to the youth of this country. I can sum it up in one word—volunteer. During my stay in Canada and my travels to the US, I was impressed by the way people there volunteered for various services. From high school students to working professionals, people volunteered their time at hospitals, old age homes, schools, etc. It was part of the routine over weekends or during summer break. When I came to India, I was surprised to see that nobody was interested in this idea of volunteering. People visited the Foundation and praised our efforts. But then what? Nothing. No one offered to volunteer their services to the Foundation. Help need not be only in the form of money. You can volunteer for a good cause and be part of the movement.

The scenario has changed over the years. Today, I get requests from students wishing to volunteer at the Foundation. I am also happy to see young people in different cities forming groups and associations to work for a cause. It is important for us to inculcate the spirit of volunteering in the next generation. The youth are often blamed for being self-centred. Volunteering is one thing that will add another dimension to their thought process. At Srikiran Hospital, we encourage the trainees to interact with the patients and understand their life stories. Once they realize that their patients are not merely cases but also humans with emotions and experiences, they understand the importance of our work here at the Foundation. It is a sort of reality check for them.

Fighting the Demons

Life at the Foundation has been a learning experience for me in more ways than one. Learning to run an organization and dealing with different people has been an outward journey. The internal journey started the day the airplane carrying my wife and children crashed.

It started with anger and bitterness and hatred towards everybody around me. I was dissatisfied with God and His unjust ways. But gradually, the bitterness gave way to questions—'Why me, why this spilling of innocent blood?' If my family and I had in any way sinned and were paying the price for it, what had all the passengers done? Had they all sinned against mankind? Did they deserve such annihilation?

Slowly, things changed. I pulled myself together. With an aim in front of me, I was able to channelize my energies in the right direction. I am thankful to God for giving me a goal to achieve at a time when I might have turned to despair or rage. As time passed, I was able to forgive them. I realized that no amount of anger will get my wife and children back. The court case against the terrorists went on for years. People often asked me why I was not following the judicial process. But I was not interested in seeing those responsible get punished for it. My only concern was the reason why it all happened. In such cases, it is important to know what led to such acts of violence, so that they are not repeated.

As a victim, I realize this much; unfortunately those involved in violence—whether causing it or suffering because of it—are caught in a cycle of vengeance. An eye for an eye and a tooth for a tooth attitude of people and governments has resulted in a lot of bloodshed and misery across the world. If we don't curb it now, if we don't learn to forgive, we will be left with a generation of humans without humanity.

The Way Forward

The Sankurathri Foundation, Sarada Vidyalayam and Srikiran Institute of Ophthalmology—all these institutions came into existence because I lost the three most important people of my life. Had they lived, I would probably not have done all this. My life would have been completely different. At this age, I would have probably retired and spent time with Manju, Srikiran, Sarada and probably my grandchildren. I don't know how that kind of life would have been. But one thing I am sure of—my children would have been brought up with the same values and ethics that I now inculcate in the students at Sarada Vidyalayam. They would have been as focused in their work and career as the doctors at Srikiran Hospital. They would have done their bit for the society by volunteering their time and energy. No matter what career path they would have chosen, their lives would have been an example of integrity and commitment. Today, the values that I wished my children would have lived by are present in every child at Sarada Vidyalayam. And that's my true legacy.

I don't see the Foundation and its work as an heirloom that should be passed onto another set of capable hands. It is not possible for any one person to manage the entire set-up and that's why we have evolved systems to ensure the smooth running of the place. There is a core team of members who understand how the Foundation works and how it should be managed. I believe in delegating work and power, and not centralizing them in one single person. My core team, trained and mentored by me, is completely capable of carrying forward my mission with a fervour that matches mine, without compromising our values.

While MSMF continues to support the hospital with its fund-raising efforts, I have realized that in the long run, the hospital needs to be self-sustaining. With the state-of-the-art facilities that we offer, Srikiran Hospital is now being looked upon as a high-quality eye care centre, and not just a charitable one. The number of paid patients coming to the hospital for treatment is increasing and we are hoping that this growing number will eventually make the hospital a self-sustaining one.

What was once my dream, has today become a mission; what was once my desire to do good, has today become a vision. With so many hands joining in the effort and so many lives benefitting from our endeavours, I am happy to see my aim has been achieved. A part of me yearns for the life that was ruthlessly stolen from me, but there's also a part of me that cherishes the ability I have today to make a difference in people's lives.

I will always miss Manju, Srikiran and Sarada. But they will continue to be with me as long as the work that is started in their names grows and improves lives. I only live with that 'Ray of Hope'.

How You Can Help

Since its inception, the Srikiran Institute of Ophthalmology has provided eye care facilities to over 1,955,230 patients in need, and performed over 191,190 cataract surgeries without charge. All this was and is only possible with the involvement of many kind philanthropists and institutions. Even after all these efforts, there are still many people who need help to improve their quality of life. In India, there is a backlog of 12 million cataracts to be operated on, and the problem is even more prominent in rural areas. Your help will be useful in maintaining the quality of service, in making services affordable as well as available, strengthening the infrastructure, and continuing to provide free service to those who are really in need.

You can donate online for specific purposes:

₹9,000/-	Educate a poor child for 1 year
₹3,000/-	One meal for 100 children per 1 day
₹3,000/-	One Cataract operation for poor patient
₹4,000/-	One day meals for 100 poor patients
₹1,50,000/-	Sponsor an eye camp for 50 surgeries

Donation to general fund – any amount

You can also become a part of us by:

- Volunteering your time and skills at the institute (depending on qualifications and experience)
- Identifying persons with eye problems and sending them to the Institute.
- Donating much- needed building materials, furniture, equipment or any other materials.
- By donating money to the corpus fund.
- Donating for cataract surgeries and sponsoring of screening clinics in a village.

*Contributions are exempted from tax in India, US and Canada.
**The Foundation has permission to receive donations from abroad under the Foreign Contribution Regulation Act.

Please come forward, we need you.

Within India, the donations can be sent to our Bank of Baroda account by online transfer to the following address.

Bank details of Sankurathri Foundation, Kakinada

Name of the Bank: Bank of Baroda
Account name: Sankurathri Foundation
Account .Number: 2786 01 0000 2239
Branch Name: Ramanayyapeta
MIRC: 533012003
IFS code: BARB0RAMPET (This is Zero, not O)

Alternatively, you could write a cheque drawn to the name of SANKURATHRI FOUNDATION, and send it to:

Managing Director
Sankurathri Foundation
A.P.S.P. Camp Post
Kakinada – 533 005
Andhra Pradesh

Tel: (0884) 230 6301
Fax: (0884) 230 6345

Bill Gibson →
＿＿＿＿＿＿

↑ Kennedy
＿＿＿＿＿＿   Tyler
                ＿＿＿＿

Kids — Taiwan Ideyen
＿＿＿＿＿＿＿＿＿＿＿＿

Genetic expert - Ancestors
   Taiwan →

  — Philippies →   [Current]
＿＿＿＿＿＿＿＿＿＿   ＿＿＿＿＿

Ding Guo — DNA test   Eva Wahl
＿＿＿＿＿＿＿＿＿＿＿＿＿   Preldin

Reconnect Jam - H.K.

Bei Ling — Chinese PEN
       ＿＿＿＿＿＿＿＿＿＿＿
" Going Home " intellect
       ＿＿＿＿＿＿＿
    wife (Trans & Bao)
    ＿＿＿＿＿＿＿＿＿＿
    Taipei